Geoffrey Durham became a
from a thirty-five year career i
in order to write about Quake
Twelve Quakers series of books, compiled an anthology *The Spirit of the Quakers* (2010), published three editions of *Being a Quaker: a guide for newcomers* (2011-2024) and written *What Do Quakers Believe?* (2019), as well as making numerous broadcasts, including two editions of *Thought for the Day* for BBC Radio 4. He is a regular speaker at Quaker events.

BEING A Quaker

A guide for newcomers

THIRD EDITION, REVISED AND UPDATED

Geoffrey Durham

DISCOVERING QUAKERS

First edition published 2011
Second edition, revised and updated, published 2013
Reprinted with minor revisions 2015
Reprinted 2016, 2017, 2019
Third edition, revised and updated, published 2024
Discovering Quakers www.discoveringquakers.org.uk
ISBN 978-1-0687482-0-2

Cover, typesetting and design by Rosamund Saunders
Cover image: Shutterstock
Printed by Henry Ling Ltd, Dorchester, UK

Contents

Part Two

Part Three

Preface

Every Quaker book written for newcomers goes out of date in a decade. The essentials of the faith don't waver, but the Quaker way of living and expressing them changes subtly all the time. These shifts are usually a result of the conscience and good sense of the Quaker community, but they occasionally come from unexpected sources.

The first edition of this book was conceived and written in 2010 and it came out a year later. Just two years on it needed an urgent update. So I prepared a new edition that took into account the response of British Quakers to the growing climate emergency. It was popular, with four new printings, and the staff at Friends House in London gave away thousands of copies free to members of the public who asked for information.

In 2020 the Covid-19 pandemic forced us all to live differently. During its first couple of weeks a large number of Quaker meetings in Britain went online. I felt confident that things would get back to normal once the nation returned to its old habits, but I was wrong. Online meetings have proliferated, so a new edition of this book has beckoned again.

Even though it was the initial spur to rewrite sections of the book, I hope I haven't given online worship undue prominence. There have been other developments: the word 'overseer' has all but disappeared from the vocabulary of British Quakers; the vital work of Woodbrooke College has moved almost exclusively online; British Quakers have changed the pattern of their annual decision-making gatherings; many books have gone out of print, causing me to revise the recommendations in the *What Next?* section; scores of other details have changed; and the original publisher, Quaker Quest Network, is no longer in operation.

As before, I must be clear that I have written this book for British readers. There are a lot of contrasts between our practices in Britain and those in parts of the USA, South America, Africa and beyond. Those who regularly attend silent meetings of the kind held in Britain now represent about 15% of the world's total. The vast majority of Quakers in North America, Kenya, Uganda, Taiwan, Bolivia, the Philippines, Peru and many other countries attend programmed meetings which are frequently based on an evangelical Christian message. So I suggest that readers wanting to know about the ways of Quakers in that tradition should put this volume straight back on the shelf and instead track down one of the excellent books written by J. Brent Bill or Thomas D. Hamm, to mention two of many.

Quakerism is an experience-based faith and much of the story of this book is inevitably my own. So it may seem odd that I refer throughout to Quakers as 'they'. I've found it necessary for two reasons. Firstly, some of the anecdotal material dates from my earliest days before I ever thought of joining the Religious Society of Friends, so 'they' is unavoidable in that context. And secondly, references in books for newcomers to 'we Quakers' have always sounded smug and self-satisfied to me. For those reasons, the 'we' of this narrative is all of us, Quaker or not. 'They' are the Quakers, whom I hope I've managed to characterise with a measure of objectivity.

In April 2012 the scientific journal *Animal Behaviour* published an article reporting that white-crowned sparrows in San Francisco now sing higher and more loudly in order to hear one another over the traffic noise on the nearby Golden Gate Bridge. In a similar way, Quakers are realising that they must adapt their approach and express themselves more clearly if they are to be understood above the racket of twenty-first century life. I hope this book may do a little to add to that understanding, and that Quakers will never stop developing new ways to speak their truth.

Acknowledgements

The first edition of this book was originally the idea of Alec Davison, a brilliant creator of Quaker projects, so my first acknowledgement and thanks must go to him. I was also privileged at that time to work with a small support group of experienced Quakers – Val Ferguson, Ingrid Greenhow and Jean Jenn – who gave me their unstinting backing and assistance with the original edition. I couldn't have done it without them.

When I was preparing that first version in 2010, some friends generously consented to write occasional paragraphs when I felt the reader needed to hear more than one voice. In putting together this latest volume, I have kept their contributions exactly as they were. In the interests of continuity, their pieces are not credited on the page, so I thank the authors warmly now: David Amos, Terri Banks, Shanthini Cawson, Anne Charvet, Val Ferguson, Trudy Hayden, Michael Hennessey, Pippa Hockton, Rachel Hope, Jean Jenn, Mary Lou Leavitt, Margot Lunnon, John Marsh, Laurie Michaelis, Alan Thomas, Ruth Tod and Sam Walton.

For the second and third editions I am grateful to a long list of friends who have helped, including some who have kindly agreed to wade through the book again and give me their comments and suggestions: Jennifer Barraclough, Helen Drewery, Ingrid Greenhow, Alistair Heslop, Jean Jenn, Kirsten Lavers, Margot Lunnon, Eoin McCarthy, Jo Muller and Janet Scott. I owe them all a great debt.

Thanks are also due to authors and publishers for permission to reproduce extracts from their work: David Boulton and Ian Kirk-Smith, former editor of *The Friend*, for David's letter published in the issue of 5th November 2010; Louisa Wright of Quaker Books and Pam Lunn for the extract from *Costing Not Less Than Everything: sustainability and spirituality in challenging times* (London: Quaker Books, 2011); Michael Hutchinson, formerly Acting Recording Clerk, for allowing quotations from *Quaker faith and practice* and the reproduction in full of *Advices and queries* (London: The Religious Society of Friends [Quakers] in Britain, 1995; 5th edition, 2013). The extract from *The True Wilderness* by H.A. Williams (London: Continuum, 3rd edition 2002) is reproduced by kind permission of Continuum International Publishing Group.

Finally, a huge thank you to the Yew Tree fund for their financial support. They represent an endowment fund of Mid Thames Area Quakers and this book would not have been published without their generosity.

Prologue

On one never-to-be-forgotten Sunday morning, I found myself one of a small company of silent worshippers who were content to sit down together without words, that each one might feel after and draw near to the Divine Presence ...

Caroline Stephen, 1890

The Quakers changed my life. That sounds like evangelism, but I'm not trying to convert you. It is a statement of fact. My initial hesitant months of attending Quaker meetings gave me spiritual fulfilment of a kind that I had never experienced until then; and now, thirty years after first walking into my local meeting house, I feel centred and alive in ways that still surprise me. I am not a better person. I still have many of the problems I had before. But I have changed. And it was being with Quakers that did it.

My discovery of Quakers began when I was in my mid-forties. I happened to notice a poster high above a wall at the side of the road. And I noticed it again – every day for three weeks, in the end – as I drove to my temporary place of work. Sitting in what became a familiar London traffic jam, I found myself looking up to my left and reading the billboard: *Peace is a process to engage in, not a goal to be reached.* At the bottom was one word: *Quakers.* It meant little to me at first, but after a few mornings of sitting in the gridlock, I began to feel it insinuating itself subtly, quietly into my head. 'Peace is a process, not a goal. But I've always thought of it as a goal, unattainable perhaps, but important to acknowledge – is that wrong? Are Quakers involved in the quest for world peace? And are they telling me to engage in that? Or perhaps they mean I should make peace part of my everyday life – but how would that work? And anyway, how is all this part of a religion?'

I knew as much about the Quakers as many people of my generation: they drove ambulances during the Second World War because they refused to be part of the fighting (only partly true, I later discovered); they won a Nobel prize for peace after the conflict because of their commitment to relief work; some of them were conscientious objectors; they believed in working for social justice; and they held their meetings in silence – again, as I was to find out shortly, not by any means the whole story.

That was it: the sum of my knowledge of a religious group who once numbered nearly one in a hundred of the British population. I didn't know how long they had been in existence or what they believed in. I wasn't even sure if they were Christian, though I was fairly certain they started that way. I was ignorant. As far as I was concerned, the Quakers were a well-meaning blank.

I determined to find out more. I looked up 'Quaker' in the phone book – there was no internet then – and discovered that their headquarters was only a couple of miles away. I slipped down there in my lunch hour. It was an imposing, impressive, unlovely building with a smiling receptionist. He directed me to a bookshop on the ground floor, where he said I would find material for newcomers.

I'm not sure what I expected: probably a small room piled high with improving pamphlets overseen by a crusty volunteer. But no, this was a revelation, a large, airy, friendly store containing the most intelligent, diverse collection of religious books I had ever seen for sale in one place. They stocked volumes on Buddhism, Hinduism, atheism and Islam; they had a whole section on Jesus, who he was historically, what he really said; I found shelf upon shelf of material about peace and peacemaking; they sold works on politics, ecology, theology and race. And hundreds of books about Quakers.

There were biographies, accounts of their early struggles as a persecuted group of religious mavericks in the seventeenth century, descriptions of their fights against slavery, accounts of their campaigns for prison reform. There was a seemingly endless number of booklets in which Quakers were speaking to each other about what it means to be a Quaker, how to live better, how to live simply, how to make a difference. And yes, there were volumes about the Friends Ambulance Unit in both world wars.

I was intrigued. I browsed for nearly an hour. Finally, I bought six slim, cheap paperbacks that looked as if they might be useful to newcomers, and went to a café across the road. I sat there for the rest of the afternoon and read them all in one go. I never made it back to work that day, a perk of the self-employed.

What makes something suddenly click? Everything I read fascinated me. It's true that I was looking for a new way of life, a place to be. But for all that, I can't quite explain the constant reverberation in my head as I devoured these books about Quakers. I read a small selection of quotations by George Fox, one of the leaders of the movement in the seventeenth century; a couple of helpful introductions to the silent meetings; a memoir by a BBC journalist who had recently discovered Quakerism; a collection of thoughts by modern Quakers of all ages and backgrounds; and lastly there was a slim red book, a leaflet almost, called *Advices and queries*. It was a list of numbered paragraphs and seemed to consist of exactly what it said on the cover – questions and advice. Some of the queries were searching ('Are you honest and truthful in all you say and do?'), others were demanding ('Do you cherish your friendships, so that they grow in depth and understanding and mutual respect?'). All of them were a challenge. But there was one particular piece of advice that really got me. The booklet opened naturally at the centre pages and two words sprang out, as if they were meant for me alone. *Live adventurously*.

I had to visit one of their meeting houses. I wanted to experience their hour of communal silence for myself. There was no set pattern to a Quaker meeting, I was learning, but there was clearly some discipline. I wondered if it was going to resemble Buddhist meditation, or a prayer meeting, or perhaps it would remind me of the church services of my childhood. I had read that people occasionally stood up to speak – maybe it was going to be like group therapy.

I discovered that there were a few meeting houses close to my home and chose one to try. I felt unaccountably nervous. Was I going to be able to sit in silence for an hour? What was I going to think about? And what, for goodness sake, was it all for?

When the day came, I waited outside the meeting house and went in at the last minute. I didn't want to talk to anyone. I thought they might try to convert me. The chairs were in a circular arrangement. I found a seat by the wall – I'm an inveterate sitter-at-the-back in unfamiliar situations – and looked around. There were perhaps eighty people in the room. Some were sitting erect, eyes closed, hands palm up on their knees. Others appeared equally relaxed in their own particular styles. A few had their eyes open, one leg crossed casually over the other, for all the world as if they were having a cup of tea with friends. All sat in stillness.

I wasn't sure where to begin, so I closed my eyes. I had thoughts that felt irreligious. Shopping, children and an infuriating client invaded my mind. I found it difficult to dig out any calm at all: these Quakers had to be achieving something that I wasn't. I was getting it wrong. Perhaps I should leave. Or maybe I could find meaning in the fact that a room full of people was agreeing to sit quietly with none of them taking the lead.

Minutes went by. I enjoyed the tranquillity. I felt composed. I knew I was thinking too much, but I wouldn't let it worry me. I wanted to savour the hour. The silence grew and deepened. Stillness began to steal on me. Maybe it was the start of what Quakers call worship – was this perhaps what I'd come for? I never found out, because from outside the window my dreamy state was interrupted by a din. A radio was playing: worse, someone was pushing up the volume. It was the airy banter of a DJ announcing Sunday morning's easy listening. But this wasn't easy. It felt like sabotage. Eyes began to open, brows began to furrow, shoes began to shuffle. To my surprise, no one left to remonstrate with the perpetrator of our loss. In fact, one or two Quakers began to smile. Louis Armstrong was singing *What a Wonderful World.*

Yet, little by little, it ceased to matter. Another spirit took over. Someone suggested that we continue in a vein of co-operation and fellowship. No one else said anything. No one needed to, because we were already searching collectively for the calm that had been snatched from us. And despite the disruption, the annoyance, the racket, we found ourselves able, against all expectation, to unite once more as a group.

Serenity returned. My eyes closed again, but this time with an appreciation that a Quaker meeting was not about individual meditation so much as a communal, joint stillness in which a group of people could reach a degree of understanding entirely separate and distinct from anything they might discover on their own. This was an experience we were all having together, and while it would have been different without the unwelcome cacophony, it wasn't necessarily worse. Personally, I became aware of a still centre in myself that I had seldom known and had never encountered without witnessing a dawn, a twilight or a seascape. And yet the radio rattled on. It was, very slightly, miraculous. I was hooked.

I went back the following week. This time, there was no interruption – in fact I've never had an experience like that first Quaker meeting in any of my hundreds of visits since. The second encounter was a good one, perhaps a little anticlimactic in comparison with the shenanigans of the week before, but an hour in which I was able to appreciate the bliss of quietness and learn just a little more about the unique dynamic of this transforming spiritual practice.

And I continue to learn today. I know now that it gets better and easier the more you do it and that the first-time experience of a newcomer is rarely a good gauge of how it may one day turn out. I understand that it has little in common with the fine sentiments I may feel when observing a beautiful landscape. And I appreciate that there can unquestionably be more to a Quaker meeting than silence. There can be love, truth, openness to the spirit and an encounter with the divine.

For the first six weeks, I never spoke to a Quaker. I left as soon as the meeting was over, because I still had a tremor of fear that someone might try to convert me. It was enough for the moment to sit with Quakers and be part of the illuminating spiritual encounters that I was sharing with them. But, for all that, I was storing up questions. How could it work with no one in charge? Where was the statement of Quaker beliefs? Did I have to be a pacifist? Did I have to join? I wasn't getting answers to these questions, because I wasn't staying long enough to ask. It was a stupid situation of my own making, but I was just too nervous and diffident to break my self-imposed deadlock.

It might have gone on like that for months, but in my seventh week a friendly Quaker broke the ice. The meeting had been a good one and I was about to make my customary dash for the exit, when the young man sitting next to me turned a little in his chair. He said, 'I've noticed you here for a few weeks now – how are you finding it?'

Well, I could hardly slope off then. So I took a breath. I summoned up the first of a growing list of my uncertainties. I said, 'I'm enjoying it,' and paused, 'but... I find it odd that there's no spiritual direction here.' He smiled and looked me straight in the eye. He said, 'Yes, it is odd, isn't it?' He didn't add anything else. He didn't explain. And suddenly, seven weeks in, I knew I wanted to stay. He hadn't said, 'Ah, that's interesting because we Quakers have no hierarchy', or 'Yes, with Quakers, spiritual direction comes from the whole meeting'. Both would have been true, but not right for me then. Instead, I'd been listened to. He hadn't tried to persuade me of anything, but there was a hint that there might be more for me to find out if I stayed. He implied new mysteries to come. And he was right, there were. And that day, for the first time, I hung on and met some Quakers.

I was struck by how open-minded and open-hearted they were. They understood that my interest in their way of life might just turn out to be one more stop along the way and they respected my spiritual path. I was able to be part of their meeting for as long as I liked, fifty years if I wanted to, and I would never be asked to join the Religious Society of Friends. They described it as being an 'attender'. And they often called me 'Friend'. I found it unnerving to begin with, but I quickly came to value it as a greeting that has been familiar to Quakers for centuries. It derives from an original name, Friends of Truth, which became the Religious Society of Friends in the eighteenth century when they introduced a system of membership. 'Quakers', on the other hand, was a derisive nickname and is older. It was coined in 1650 by a judge, Gervase Bennet, in an attempt to make fun of the Quaker he was accusing of blasphemy. The Quakers, having a dry and defiant sense of humour, chose to adopt it publicly for themselves and have used it ever since. So 'Friend' and 'Quaker' are identical and interchangeable today. To avoid confusion, I have decided almost always to use the word 'Quaker' in this book.

The more I learned, the more interested I became in what Quakers had to say. I asked questions. I took part in endless conversations. I earwigged as other newcomers made their enquiries. I once overheard a brief exchange which, having been brought up an Anglican, I found fascinating: it revealed in a short time so much about Quakers' absence of fixed religious thinking. A visitor was asking a member, 'Do Quakers believe that Jesus was the son of God?' 'Oh yes,' he replied, 'and so are you and so am I.' It was an eye-opener for me. It would have been of no interest at all, of course, to someone whose upbringing had not been Christian, and yet I quickly came to realise that people of Buddhist, Jewish, Baha'i, Jain and many other religious backgrounds were coming to meetings, finding they liked them and asking questions. And, like me, some were staying. There were also folk who had difficulty using the word 'God', preferring other terms used by Quakers, such as 'the Light', 'the Truth', 'the Seed', 'the Eternal' and 'the Life', to express what they were experiencing. Then again, others were declaring themselves to be nontheists – not 'atheist', that doesn't describe their position – because their experience made it difficult for them to accept the concept of God as a supernatural power, though at the same time their reverence for the life force, for nature, for humanity, was finding expression in the ways of Quakers. I also came across Christians of many traditions, some believing, as the early Quakers did, in the divinity of Jesus, others regarding him as an enlightened human whose message of love and truth had become the centre of their lives.

How is it possible to unite these differing customs, faiths and understandings? The key, I came to realise, is to be found in one question buried in the seventh of the *Advices and queries* (the booklet printed in full as Appendix 2 of this book): 'Are you open to new light, from whatever source it may come?' As a form of words it is less than a century old, but as a principle of the Quaker faith it has been there from the very beginning. Quakers have always honoured and valued the journeys of others and accepted that, as George Fox put it in the seventeenth century, 'though the way seems to thee diverse... yet all are but one in the end'. The early Quakers were Christians because they lived in a Christian country: if they had lived in the multi-faith society we inhabit today, it might have been different. In twenty-first century Britain, Quaker communities, which anyone can be a part of by just attending regularly, are all distinct from one other and all unique. The life experience, character and faith of their participants make them that way. And if a person's circumstances, feelings or belief take them elsewhere, their Quaker friends will be the first to understand. It could hardly be any other way, because in most cases that was what brought them to Quakerism in the first place.

As I continued to attend meetings and learn about Quakers, I began to understand that they can't claim to agree – and don't want to agree – a set roster of beliefs shared by them all. They talk together, work communally and influence each other, without needing to present a consistently united front or intone the same thing in unison at the same time. So there's no creed, no dotted line that you have to sign, no questionnaire. Quakers welcome people of every background and faith, every gender, every sexual orientation. They enjoy diversity and celebrate the equality of us all. Their decisions are taken in a unique way that does away with majority voting. They are content to disagree on matters of belief and will often tell each other about it: plainly, distinctly and without malice. They know one other well and share their spiritual lives in a way that allows them to find unity in the sheer stimulus of it all. Individual experience is what matters. Difference does not have to mean discord.

But there's a strong tendency among Quakers to keep themselves to themselves, not wanting to evangelise or persuade the world that they are right. It's admirable in its intention, but it leads inevitably to confusion in the minds of the public. Many people, knowing about their religious liberalism, think of them as woolly-minded and difficult to pin down. Others fancy they are an evangelical sect. There are Christian critics who accuse Quakers of being heretics who deny the sacraments. Still more are sure that Quakers must have died out. My own view is that all these perceptions are mistaken, and I hope to show why later in this book.

I'm not a Quaker spokesperson – there's no such thing – so it's unavoidable that much of what I say will be drawn from my own experience and enthusiasms. But in talking about what happened to me, I won't be suggesting that it will necessarily be the same for you. When I know that my viewpoint is not widely shared, or in areas where there are different shades of opinion and knowledge, I'll be quoting from other Quakers. My aim is to cover the ground and give as wide a perspective as possible so that you can make up your own mind. And since Quakers are often indistinct when they talk about themselves, I'll close this prologue by making some observations about them that I hope will be clear, objective and helpful.

Most Quakers of my acquaintance believe that every person can have a direct, unmediated relationship with a life-force that some of them choose to call God. They accept that people who open themselves to it may find themselves impelled to work for personal and social change. They try to conduct their affairs in openness to the divine spirit, but are none the less rigorous in examining the plans of Quakers who feel moved by God to take action, because they know from experience that ego can sometimes be involved. When something is wrong, they speak plainly about it. They value wisdom and experience over privilege and power, and believe in the importance of truth and integrity in everything.

Most Quakers are uncomfortable with statements of religious certainty. They joyfully embrace uncertainty and regard it as a positive element in their spiritual lives. Uncertainty, however, does not mean an absence of shared understanding. Every Quaker I know trusts in what they call 'that of God' in everyone. It follows that they also all believe in the equality – not sameness, just utter equality – of every human being on the planet. So they try to base their actions, beliefs and opinions on that principle. They accept that conflict is bound to happen, but reject violence as a way of solving it, preferring instead always to seek peaceful means. They do what they can to live simply. They consider the world's environmental emergency to be a spiritual and religious crisis as well as a practical one, and they try to behave in ways that show reverence for the earth.

These are not creeds, but observations of my own based on experience. I'll go on to talk about them fully later. If you want to learn more now, have another look at *Advices and queries*, the booklet I bought in my lunch hour thirty years ago. There you will find in paragraph 28 a phrase that seems to me to say more about Quakers in seven words than many books manage in a hundred times that number. *Attend to what love requires of you*. It is a major impetus behind the thinking and behaviour of Quakers. It gives them meaning and purpose. It fires them to work for peace and social justice. And it is the starting point of an adventure in the spirit which has changed millions of lives. My hope in writing this book is to shine a light along your way.

Part One

Stand still in that power which brings peace.

George Fox, 1652

What is a Quaker Meeting?

'Meeting' means everything to Quakers. There are meetings for worship, meetings for business and meetings for clearness. When a Quaker marries, it's a meeting for worship for marriage; when a Quaker dies, they call it a memorial meeting. Their annual conference is a yearly meeting. A small group of Quakers is described as a local meeting and that meeting often holds its meetings in the meeting room of a meeting house. They don't own churches, chapels or temples, nor do they hold services. Everything is a meeting. At first sight it's confusing.

Take it slowly, though, and the mists begin to clear. Quakers' use of the word has logic on its side. What matters most to them, after all, is personal experience. No one directs Quaker events. They are not rituals, ceremonies or services. Each is a unique coming together of minds, bodies and souls. Calling these communal encounters 'meetings' makes sense. They are shared collectively by everyone.

Quaker groups which meet together regularly are also called 'meetings'. The reasoning is the same: these are people who know each other well, whose lives are often linked by the beliefs they share and who spend a lot of time together. So the Quakers in Brighton, say, are collectively known as 'Brighton Meeting'. When they choose to assemble for devotion and prayer, they hold a meeting for worship. As they set off from home, they may say to their loved ones, 'I'm going to meeting'.

In many cases, the event will take place in a meeting house that was built for the purpose. Quakers don't consecrate these buildings or regard them as especially hallowed. They are often beautiful to look at and many of them are greatly loved, but none of them has ever been blessed or declared ceremonially to be a centre of worship. Quaker groups that don't own a property usually meet in a community centre or hall, or sometimes a private house. One group I know meets in a small theatre.

Most Quakers believe that there is no difference between the sacred and the secular. All days are precious, as holy as each other. So it follows that they do not celebrate a Sabbath. They hold their meetings for worship at times that are convenient for their particular group. That usually means a gathering every Sunday, since it's time off for most people. In some towns Quakers also hold midweek meetings at lunchtime and during the evening. Traditional festivals such as Christmas, Passover, Easter or Diwali are not considered to be of greater spiritual significance than other days, so Quakers give them no special emphasis. Many enjoy family celebrations at home on those occasions, but they don't feel the need to grace the day with any particular religious message.

A good number of Quakers and newcomers have difficulty gaining access to these meetings, of course – either because their nearest Quaker venue is too far away, or as a result of a disability. They now have an alternative that began to emerge in the early 2020s: meetings that use video conferencing to bring groups of worshippers together in a virtual space. There are hundreds of these meetings worldwide. Most are attached to long-established Quaker groups; others began originally as pop-ups but are now firmly fixed in the Quaker calendar. Quakers call them 'online' or 'virtual' meetings, to distinguish them from the more traditional 'in-person' or 'face-to-face' meetings.

In the following sections, I hope to explain in detail how meetings for worship work in both these forms, and why they affect people deeply, in some cases helping them to take life-changing decisions. I'll go on to clarify the ways in which groups of Quakers run their affairs with no one in charge. I'll describe how the pattern of the meeting for worship is used for the creation of common policy. Then in the final pages of Part One, I'll explain how it is also used for weddings and funerals.

Finding a meeting that works for you

If you want to know more about Quakers, a good first step is to take part in a meeting for worship.

If you want to go to an in-person meeting in the traditional way, go to the British Quaker website (www.quaker.org.uk) and you'll find your nearest meeting place by typing in your postcode. If you're in any doubt about the time the meeting for worship starts or the best options for public transport, a quick phone call to the listed contact person should sort everything out.

If you'd rather go to an online meeting it's still a good idea to get in touch with the contact person at your nearest meeting, just to find out if they run one. If so, you'll be told the time to log on and then be sent the link in the usual way. Alternatively, you could go to: www.woodbrooke.org.uk/worship/#worship-timetable. At the time of writing, that is the link to the online meetings run by Woodbrooke, an international Quaker learning and research organisation based in the UK. They run around ten online meetings each week and so there should be one at least that will suit your timetable. And the Discovering Quakers website boasts a timetable of online meetings throughout the world. You'll find it at https://www.discoveringquakers.org.uk/online-meetings-for-worship

In the next few sections I'll explain what happens in an in-person meeting. I'll give details about online meetings in How Online Quaker Meetings Work later in Part One; however, if you're thinking of attending one, I do urge you to read the following few pages about in-person meetings first, because just about everything that happens during a meeting in a physical room also applies to the 'virtual' Quaker experience, even though the detail may not be exactly the same.

Going to an In-person Meeting

If you've read the Prologue, you may remember that I was nervous when I walked into my first meeting. I think most people are. But my experience has been that those nerves quickly disappear as the stillness of the Quaker experience takes over.

When you arrive, you may come across someone offering to shake your hand as you walk through the door. It's common practice at many meetings and is not reserved for newcomers – everyone who comes is greeted at the door. It's useful, because if you want to ask questions, read a leaflet, or look round the building, your welcomer can point you in the right direction. Many people, of course, prefer to be left alone on the first day. If you're one of them – I certainly was – I suggest you go straight to the room where the worship is to be held and take a seat anywhere you like. The meeting begins when the first person sits down, so there's no announcement to indicate that everything is suddenly under way. By the agreed starting time, just about everyone will have arrived – it's not a good idea to be late if you can help it, because you'll miss something – and those particular people assembled at that particular time on that particular day will have begun to share their own collective religious experience.

The room will be set out with seats forming a circle or square, so that everyone can see everyone else. In the oldest meeting houses, there are often two permanent banks of seating facing one another. The layout always emphasises the communal nature of worship. In the centre, there will be a small table. It may have flowers on it. And there will be books, too. A Bible is usually there, and possibly one or two key texts from non-Christian religions, together with a pair of specifically Quaker works that are always found: *Advices and queries* (Appendix 2 of this book) and a much-loved volume called *Quaker faith and practice.*

Quaker faith and practice is an essential text. You can read it in full online (qfp.quaker.org.uk) or buy it in book form. It gives Quakers information and advice on holding their meetings and running their affairs, but that is only the beginning. It also comprises a collection of extracts, paragraphs and sentences written by Quakers over the last three and a half centuries that I and many others have found to be uniquely valuable and inspiring. There are chapters on personal journeys, close relationships and living faithful lives; you can read passages on peacemaking and social responsibility; one section, entitled 'Reflections', has become a source of spiritual nurture to large numbers of Quakers who make time to read from it every day. It is a treasury of wisdom and hope. Unusually for the core work of a religious group, the whole book is re-compiled from scratch every thirty years or so, ensuring that it remains contemporary and relevant to each new generation.

These books are not intended to be read throughout the meeting. They are on the table for anyone who feels a need to refer to them. If you want to spend time exploring *Quaker faith and practice*, or indeed any other Quaker books, you'll be able to borrow them from the meeting's library afterwards. For the moment, I suggest you simply sit in the gathering silence with the people who have joined you. You might want to look around and see who your companions will be for the next hour. Or perhaps you prefer to sit with your eyes closed and settle into the tranquillity.

If you're familiar with transcendental or Buddhist meditation, your experience may come in useful in the process of 'centring down', as Quakers call it. Accomplished meditators often say that the techniques and mantras they have learned through their discipline are essential to them as they settle in the silence, and I'll have more to say about that later. For the moment, though, I think it's important to be clear that most Quakers doubt whether meditation, even as a group event, has much in common with the meeting for worship itself. Outwardly, of course, they are similar – in fact, someone looking at them objectively might find it hard to tell the difference – but from the inside, they feel entirely distinct. The principal reason only takes a moment's thought: it's possible to meditate alone, whereas, self-evidently, a Quaker meeting involves more than one person. It has to be shared. And it also carries with it an authority, an inevitable series of consequences and results – again, I'll come to these shortly – which only serve to emphasise that comparisons don't work. There are a lot of Quakers who find meditation to be an important part of their lives, but few who mistake it for their meeting for worship.

It can also be a temptation to assume that silence is the purpose of a Quaker meeting, that thinking your own thoughts and not saying anything for an hour is going to constitute a religious experience. That may happen, of course, and it may turn out to be a refreshing change and, who knows, you may be delighted by the opportunity to enjoy the mental space it affords, but most people agree, I think, that it isn't really what a Quaker meeting is for. After all, as with meditation, you could do it on your own at home. One of the joys of sitting with others is the simple fact of their presence and their active participation. Silence is certainly an important ingredient in what is going on, but it isn't the point. I see it as an aid to what a Quaker meeting is really about, which is the mutual realisation of a collective stillness. When that is felt by everyone in the room, truths may be revealed to them.

Silence is not the only aid to the stillness. There is another, and that, ironically, is speech. Sometimes a person attending the meeting – it can be anybody, not necessarily a Quaker – is moved to speak from a deep, unfamiliar place inside them. Their words may be incisive or uncertain, but however they emerge they will pierce the silence and give new direction to the worship. As long as there's no self-regard in the person's decision to speak – that has to be a given – what they say will contribute to the communal stillness. It's never a prepared speech and it's always intended for the meeting as a whole; an insight is unlikely to hit home if it means something only to the person who has had it. Often, it will be followed in time by one or more spoken offerings from other people in the room. Sometimes they form a pattern, so that the occasion begins to acquire a thematic shape of its own.

When someone is moved to stand and speak in a meeting, what they say is called 'ministry'. It's a rare gift that doesn't come often to most of us. Some people minister once in a lifetime, others a few times a year at most. It isn't usual to come across a person who makes a regular habit of getting to their feet, and it would be worrying if it were, because moderation is an important part of a meeting for worship.

Three established customs are worth bearing in mind. Firstly, Quakers suggest that spoken contributions are kept short, if possible. Secondly, they ask for a period of silence after someone has ministered, so that everyone can properly absorb what has just been said. (There are few things more cheerless than hearing someone rise to speak as soon as another person has sat down: not only has the meeting not had a chance to digest the last contribution, but the new speaker hasn't either, so things are certain to become disjointed.) Thirdly, people are requested not to speak more than once in a meeting – two or three times, and it starts to feel like preaching. And Quakers have a strong dislike of preaching.

The combination of silence and speech makes each Quaker meeting unique. And if an hour turns out to be totally silent, it will also have an atmosphere, character and depth all its own: the spiritual teaching absorbed in a meeting for worship doesn't necessarily come from the mouths of other people. Since meetings are by their nature unpredictable, some will inevitably be more satisfying than others, and all Quakers treasure memories of the gatherings that have resonated most deeply for them personally, the ones through which they have learned and grown. The best Quaker meetings have a formidable power, often engendered by a sense that the spirit of each person is melding into a communal stillness that is so intense, so deep-reaching it can almost be touched. Quakers have an expression for these most highly charged encounters. They call them 'gathered meetings'. They regard them as an essential part of their religious experience. An American Quaker, Thomas Kelly, wrote in 1940, 'What is the ground and foundation of the gathered meeting? In the last analysis, it is, I am convinced, the Real Presence of God.' If he is right – and I think he is – then what Quakers are doing in their meetings is waiting on the divine.

Most meetings close after about an hour, though lunch-time and evening meetings are often shorter. Two Quakers, appointed in advance by the group, shake hands when they feel the time has come to bring the meeting to a conclusion. Their handshake is a signal for everyone to follow suit and in a matter of seconds the whole room has become wreathed in smiles and greetings. It can be quite a responsibility to know the right moment to finish. The clock plays a big part in the decision, of course, but so do good sense, discernment and sensitivity to the needs of those present, so if a meeting doesn't end exactly when you thought it might, you shouldn't necessarily be surprised. Three centuries ago, Quaker meetings were open-ended, often lasting three hours and more. It's rare to encounter such extensive devotions now, but some groups hold quiet days with longer meetings. If you enjoy the power of Quaker worship, you might like to try one. They can achieve great depth.

Led by the Spirit

Gathered meetings are an essential part of Quakerism and the reason that I and so many others have found ourselves unable to stay away. They offer the possibility of deep religious experiences, of encounters with the Spirit that other denominations use symbols to express. They have the capacity to transform those who attend them. There is a mystical quality to a gathered meeting which makes it appear to be untouched by time. People's selfish thoughts dematerialise. They are able to listen. They give thanks. They discover clear ways forward. Decisions can be taken. Projects become feasible. From the outside, gathered meetings appear to be no different from any other Quaker event; for those taking part, they can be the impetus for spiritual renewal and lasting change.

In a magazine article quoted in *Quaker faith and practice*, Thomas R. Bodine wrote:

> *As a meeting 'gathers' ... there gradually develops a feeling of belonging to a group who are together seeking a sense of the Presence. The 'I' in us begins to feel like 'we'. At some point – it may be early in the meeting or it may be later, or it may never occur at all – we suddenly feel a sense of unity, a sense of togetherness with one another and with that something outside ourselves that we call God.*

It is impossible to know which meetings will gather and which will not: there seem to be few, if any, common factors. It certainly helps if those attending arrive in a spirit of preparedness, because they will need to be open to the unexpected. As they stare down the issues in their lives, worshippers are surprised by perceptions that arrive unbidden.

Ideas bubble up into the mind like spring water, exhilarating and fresh. They may be religious insights or impulses to take action. Often, they are both at once. They can be difficult to grasp at the time, but they prove equally hard to resist and soon become firm and unstoppable. Quakers have a word for their spiritually inspired resolutions. They call them 'leadings'. Leadings can bring about a big project for social justice, an alteration in a person's family dynamic, or a private decision to change one's behaviour. Large-scale or small, they are a fact of Quaker life.

Obeying the promptings of the Spirit in this way is a key part of the Quaker experience – and 'experience' is the vital word. Everything in Quakerism is based on it. If you don't have a list of set beliefs, if you turn your back on dogma, all you have to give is what you know in your heart. And the process is circular: it's because you've had insights as a direct result of your religious experience that you are able to discern that someone else's doctrine may not be for you. That's why Quakers refuse to entertain the idea of a leader handing down creeds or imperatives: they believe only what has been shown to them in practice. Gathered meetings play a crucial role in this. They awaken perception. They offer intense spiritual encounters in which people can see who they are and through which they are inspired to become who they can be.

Being Part of a Meeting for Worship

So I sit on my chair in silence with, say, ten, twenty, two hundred other people. There is no altar to look at, no crucifix, no statue, no star, no stained glass. What do I do?

It took me a while to establish my own little ways in a

Quaker meeting. When I started, I found it difficult to banish the mundane thoughts of a man with a family, a worrier with a job. But I practised. It slowly became easier to focus on what I was there for. In the early days, I had no idea what to do with my hands. Should they be palm up, thumb touching second finger? Or perhaps they would be better facing downwards, relaxed in a loose fist, gently resting on my knees? And what of my feet – square to the floor? And my eyes? Open, shut? It was all for me to decide, because there are no rules or recommended best practice.

After a month or two, I began to notice that many experienced Quakers vary what they do and I tried it. I started the meeting by looking round to see who was there, enjoying their presence and allowing it to calm me. I closed my eyes and began, as Quakers put it, to centre down. I found it helpful to say the same thing, slowly and repeatedly to myself. I chose the word 'maranatha', because it was used by one or two Christian meditators of my acquaintance who found it worked for them. It is a phrase in the ancient Aramaic language, meaning 'Oh Lord, come'. I simply borrowed it from my friends on the principle that if it was good enough for them, it was good enough for me. It helped me to clear my mind and take my brain away from the focus of my own thinking. I also liked what it meant. After a while, though, I began to feel foolish speaking a language I had no knowledge of, so I changed my mantra. I began to say the Christian 'Our Father' prayer, which I had been taught in my childhood. I recited it to myself slowly, one phrase at a time. It was a good development, because now I knew what I was saying.

Sometimes I failed to reach the end of my prayer and it didn't matter. The mantra guided my spirit to another place and I was able to let go of my own ego. If thoughts rushed in, I was usually able to set them gently to one side without allowing them to get on top of me. And what I did then, though I realise it sounds undisciplined and irreligious, was daydream. I allowed my mind to drift. There was a difference, though, between contemplation in a Quaker meeting and thinking pretty thoughts. My Quaker reverie was grounded in where I was, and why I was there. And, crucially, it wasn't going to continue for the whole hour; because if it worked I was going to be able to move on to a place of spiritual safety in which I could see myself as I really was, with humility and understanding. I was going to reach a point at which I might be open to the Spirit.

The first Quakers used to call this process 'standing in the Light'. George Fox, the pioneer of Quakerism whose works I now prize so much, wrote about it frequently. 'Stand still in that which shows and discovers,' he said – 'discovers' having the meaning of 'uncovers' in the English of the seventeenth century – and I have indeed found that the process of being still and opening myself to God has changed me. It has shown me to myself, uncovered me, and allowed me to take on challenges of a kind that I wouldn't have been able to manage before. In the gathered stillness of Quaker meetings, I've become capable of understanding simple truths about my behaviour, and I've been shown ways to take life-changing decisions.

Perhaps the most useful thing to say about how to 'be' in a Quaker meeting is that it can change over time. After many months of sitting with my eyes firmly shut I found that I no longer always needed to do that. I could begin to engage in my spiritual practice with the conscious help of those around me. And in a similar way, I found after a year or two that I didn't always want to use the mantra. So I've gradually developed a way of going straight into my daydream of the spirit. I sit on the chair with both feet on the floor, hands loosely on my lap, and I open myself to whatever may come. I'm a little better at avoiding distractions now. That has come through acknowledging that it is not an 'anything goes' process for me. There has to be a procedure to the way I behave in a Quaker meeting, some kind of discipline. If there isn't, I can easily get into a habit of wondering what's for lunch.

There are as many ways of being in a Quaker meeting as there are Quakers. Mine may not be right for you. So I have asked some friends to jot down a few words about their experience. This is what they have written.

I like to be well grounded with both feet on the floor, back well supported by the chair and hands lying gently in my lap. I close my eyes and try to move my attention from head to 'heart', which I envisage as centrally placed within my ribcage. I let all thoughts and words flutter away. They fly back, of course, but I try not to pay attention to them. Sometimes I achieve complete stillness, often I don't. When thoughts are troublesome I find any passage from Advices and queries *helps me to focus again.*

I find that it is the senses which tend to distract, so to start with I concentrate on one sense – listening. I listen to the tummy rumbles, the coughs and the creaks. I am aware of the meeting. I let the listening be wide. It spreads around me reaching farther and farther outward like water on a flat surface. Eventually, sometimes, it partakes of that silence from which all sound emanates.

I like to sit facing sunlight through the high window and settle myself in the chair in an upright comfortable position. I look around the circle and offer a smile of greeting to those I know and to those I have not yet met. Mindful of these people present I give attention to inner awareness, of being attentive and becoming open to promptings, insights or guidance.

I find it impossible to really clear my mind of everything. I am aware of the ticking of the clock, the grain of the wood in the benches, the stillness of the room. In Advices and queries *I find some words which seem to blend with my thoughts and focus me, and then I find myself going into a deeper place where I am no longer aware of the noise of the traffic outside, but become a part of the tranquillity inside.*

Arriving at the meeting house in good time, preferably without the distractions of conversation with others, driving in an unhurried way, is a great help. I often use a mantra to help me to centre down, coupled with careful breathing. It's the verse from Psalm 46, 'be still and know that I am God', which then develops into 'be still', with 'be' in my mind as I breathe in, and 'still' as I exhale.

When I sit down I immediately start to focus on things that have been on my mind – mostly trivial little tasks or worries – and then mentally peel them away, like the layers of an onion, and push them away from me, until I reach a space that is empty and quiet. At that point, I begin to 'hear' the silence and feel the stillness, and then I wait to see what will happen. It doesn't always work.

It feels like the kinks coming out of the cable on an appliance like a grass-cutter. I never seem to get fast at it. I am fairly philosophical about how long it takes, and regard the sifting of what comes up as a form of worship. Struggling really doesn't help. The nearest I have to a tip is that I sometimes try to minimise the occurrence of the word 'I' in my thoughts. What sometimes happens is that a thought starts as a strictly private preoccupation. As the meeting goes on it becomes less personal, it seems also to come from a version of myself in which brain and heart and insight unite.

I've given up trying not to think – so I let the thoughts ramble gently without trying to think them through – and in time they die out and I sometimes become truly 'still' and I later come out of a phase of what felt like timelessness, yet a connection to God and to those present. Sometimes the thoughts become a serious thread that seems to go somewhere before dying away. Then may come back later with force demanding to be considered as ministry – especially if it seems to belong in the pattern of other ministry.

The last friend mentions ministry and hints at a private decision-making process that may engage her as she turns over the messages entering her mind. It happens sooner or later to everyone who attends meetings. 'This idea in my head – is it ministry? Is it for me alone to enjoy and learn from, or is it for the whole meeting? Why is it for the whole meeting? Should I stand up and say it? Will I be able to? Will I remember what it was? Does it have any relevance to what has already been said?'

As we've already seen, Quakers are quite clear that ego must never be involved in the impulse to speak in a meeting for worship. In fact, if you find yourself with a strong desire to say something, it might be worth looking carefully at your motives: wanting to minister and actually finding yourself on your feet with words coming out of your mouth are different experiences. Almost everyone who has spoken in a Quaker meeting reports a sensation of simply having to do it. Often, there's a feeling that this is against one's will, that there is no option but to stand and say what has to be said in order to be able to sit down again. Ministering in a meeting for worship is not always a comfortable experience.

Receiving ministry, hearing it, can sometimes present a challenge if what is being said appears not to fit with what is already in the listener's mind. When I can't appreciate or understand a spoken message, I've found that the best thing I can do is simply to lay the ministry aside in my mind for the moment, not to allow it to bug me, and to accept instead that I may understand it in time. It helps me to remember not to judge each piece of ministry in isolation, but to recognise that there may be a pattern emerging that I have yet to absorb. If it was meant for somebody else in the meeting, all may become clear when they rise to speak a few minutes later.

Usually, ministry consists of an inspired observation, a thought, a memory or perhaps a reading. Sometimes the speaker will knit together the apparently unconnected ideas from two or three previous offerings. And it is not always speech. Quakers are clear that often the most important ministry comes from the participants who remain faithfully silent throughout the meeting.

Some of the most valuable contributions I've heard have been musical. I vividly remember a meeting held in a centuries-old meeting house in a small Yorkshire town. I was fairly new and visiting this group of Quakers for the first time. The gathering was silent for forty minutes. The glow of morning light through the small, high windows cast long, golden patterns onto the stone floor. The place felt hallowed. A woman stood. In a bluesy contralto, she improvised a soaring anthem of adoration to her god. No one made a sound for the rest of the hour. I'll remember those goose bumps for ever.

Nor shall I forget the two-year-old boy who walked into a less than fruitful meeting – oh, they happen – twenty minutes before its end, found a pile of *Advices and queries* by the door and wove his way unsteadily around the chairs, handing each of us a copy. He took the trouble to open them all at the centre pages (*live adventurously*) and unknowingly quickened an occasion that was in danger of sinking. He wasn't aware of what he was doing. His primary motive was play. But I can't escape the thoughts that no one ever plans good ministry, that laughter is a fine antidote to solemnity and, crucially, that a message can and will come from any of the participants in a meeting, however much they may appear to lack experience.

Taking Care

Anybody can walk into a meeting of Quakers and join them. Anybody can stand up in the stillness and say something. It might surprise you – it amazes me – how few newcomers use the occasion to deliver a sermon, a speech or a rant. It happens, of course, but rarely. When it does, Quakers have effective ways of dealing with it and I'll go on to explain some of those a little later. Much more common than a meeting being hijacked by a first-timer is the subtle damage that can sometimes be caused by someone who attends regularly and unwittingly makes an error of judgement. So in this section, I hope to explain one or two of the more familiar pitfalls. And I'll start with my own behaviour.

When I'd been attending Quaker meetings for about a year and a half, I spent six weeks working in a town a few hundred miles from my home. I visited the meeting there every Sunday. These new Quakers were warm and welcoming. It took forty minutes to drive to the meeting house and I enjoyed the unhurried journeys. I used the time to prepare myself mentally for the silent worship that was to come. I sometimes allowed my mind to wander as I drove. One day, my daydreaming led to a thought that struck me as possibly original. It doesn't matter now what the idea was, but I found a form of words that seemed to me to express it well. I felt that my little nugget had an element of wisdom about it and I was pleased. I even allowed myself to wonder whether, if the subject of it did ever happen to come up in a meeting for worship, it might possibly be suitable as ministry.

I arrived. I went into the meeting. I sat with my thought, my perceptive little insight, and let it work in my brain. The silence deepened. Nobody spoke. I asked myself if I should perhaps stand and say what was in my mind. It was well shaped now, my piece of spiritual self-help, a neat and original form of words that gave me an understanding that I hadn't had before. I wondered if it might be of use to others. I knew that Quakers went through a brief mental process to ascertain whether or not the message they had was just for themselves or for the meeting as a whole and I asked myself that question. I decided this was for the meeting. After all, it was helping me, so logically it might be of interest to them. I decided to stand. And as I prepared to rise to my feet, a woman on the other side of the room got up, paused and delivered a helpful piece of ministry.

I felt thwarted. My plan hadn't worked. I tried to get calm again. My heart began to slow down. And as I relaxed once more, I had a further thought. My piece of ministry was not that different from hers, the themes were similar. With a little adaptation, my contribution could add something to what had already been spoken. Perhaps I should say it. I should leave it a few minutes, though, because that's what Quakers do. I worked out my new delivery and prepared to stand. And as I was about to rise, it happened again. It was a man this time. He stood up slowly and what he said followed the theme of the first ministry, taking it into a new realm altogether. He closed with a short quotation from *Quaker faith and practice.* He sat. Ten minutes went by. Nobody said anything. I wondered whether to speak. After all, what I had to say was still along the same lines. In fact, the subject matter was almost identical and it made sense with what had gone before.

For the third time, I prepared to speak. And of course you're ahead of me now, you know what's coming. But I didn't. I was oblivious. I felt a deep need to say what I had to say to these people, because I thought it might help. I was sincere. And as I got ready to speak, the third contributor rose. Deftly and inspiringly, she tied together the last two pieces of ministry in a short statement that combined perceptiveness with discernment. No more needed to be said. No more was said. I'd been silenced, but nobody had known. And at last I got the message. In my head, I had been holding one meeting; in the room, the Quakers had been holding another. The two had been on parallel lines, thematically similar, but utterly separate in spirit. My problem was that I wanted to say something. But *what I want* has no contribution to make to a Quaker meeting, however public-spirited I may feel. *What I want* will get in the way. Meetings are unpredictable. They are moved by something inside people and yet at the same time mystically beyond them. And it was, I'm sure, something outside me that made certain that I didn't speak that day.

The problem I had, of course, was with my ego: I wanted to speak from a misguided need to prove to myself and others that I was wise. But it isn't only those kinds of damaging impulse that can be troublesome to Quaker worship: the simple desire for self-esteem can be just as disconcerting if, as I've seen happen, meetings for worship get confused in people's minds with psychoanalytic techniques. I once knew a man who had long been a patient in the kind of group therapy that encourages participants to talk about their problems in a safe environment. He began to worship with Quakers and felt at home. The two practices seemed similar to him (in both, after all, he was sitting in a circle with people who were free to speak without any apparent direction or programme), so he understandably found it difficult to distinguish between them. Week after week, he stood up in the stillness, expounding at length about problems he was having in his life, difficulties in his marriage, trouble at work. It helped him, but the religious life of those silent meetings began to suffer. They were being used as something they weren't intended for. They lacked spiritual energy. They became mundane, predictable and flat.

In this case the crisis, I'm pleased to say, was short-lived. Our friend had the insight and humility to realise that his views of Quaker meetings were mistaken. He began to appreciate that ministry is, to quote Marrianne McMullen in *Quaker faith and practice*, 'what is on one's soul, and it can be in direct contradiction to what is on one's mind'. He started to enjoy silent meetings for the deep spiritual insights that they offer and eventually found a life for himself among Quakers, seeking help for his psychological difficulties elsewhere. It was a fortunate outcome. There are people, of course, who lack that kind of self-awareness, perhaps as a result of illness, and who find themselves overwhelmed by a pressing need to express publicly what is going on for them. When this happens, Quakers are sympathetic and do what they can to respond with care, tenderness and love.

Another danger is that a worshipping group may latch onto an idea and minister it into the ground. Early in my Quaker life, I attended a meeting in which twelve people out of about fifty, standing in quick succession, spoke about their individual conceptions of God. Many of them had fascinating things to report, but they were telling, not responding. They were delivering their own spirit, rather than being open to a greater one. And there were just too many of them. Afterwards, I was at a loss to know how to take this overblown mixture of conjecture and conviction. I asked an experienced Quaker what he had thought. 'It was certainly a problem,' he said, 'but don't worry about it unduly. It happens sometimes – rather like the sales force suddenly being given the opportunity to talk about the product.'

Quaker groups respond to the needs of individuals for self-expression, self-care and self-esteem and they actively support them. However, if meetings for worship look at first sight like forums, or discussion groups, or opportunities for spiritual opinions to be expressed, it is an illusion. Those kinds of event are often programmed by Quaker groups and frequently prove to be helpful, but they don't have a part to play in a meeting for worship. If I'm reading a book, or remembering something I heard on the radio last week, or admiring the flowers on the table, I'm doing something entirely understandable that many people do in a Quaker meeting, but I'm not listening. I'm not doing what the meeting is for, which is opening myself to the promptings of love and truth in my heart, hearing them and responding to the challenges they present to me. Quaker meetings are about listening and waiting. They are about finding a response together.

I'm often asked what happens to someone for whom 'finding a response together' is anathema. After all, Quakers are a peace-loving fellowship with many shared concerns about violence, prejudice and conflict resolution: supposing a racist turns up, or a member of a fascist group, or a homophobe, what then? The answer is that it's unlikely to be an easy time for anyone, but that people who can't accept Quakers' understanding of equality as a religious principle are simply not going to stay long. No one will ask them to leave, but they will gain nothing by hanging around. They won't be able to railroad or force through business decisions, because the ways in which Quakers go about their affairs are slow, deliberate and thoughtful, valuing the conscience of everyone present. And so they will have to make a choice. Some things in Quakerism are not negotiable: one is the knowledge that each of us is unique, precious and a child of God.

How Online Quaker Meetings Work

Quaker worship online works in much the same way as it does in a face-to-face meeting, so – it's worth repeating – it will help you to read the previous sections before starting on this one.

In 2020, as the Covid-19 pandemic became life-threatening, all religious gatherings held in person were banned by law. Quakers lost no time in making changes and within a short time a good half of the Quaker meetings in Britain went online. Many people found the technology confusing at first, but they were soon embracing it and acknowledging this new form of worship as a godsend. A lot of Quaker meetings continue to use online meetings in addition to the face-to-face ones, so it may help you to know how they work.

It takes a little imagination at first to accept that the faces on the screen are a worshipping community, but I've been surprised by how quickly most people get used to it. Just as with an in-person meeting, seeing who's there and enjoying their presence can have a calming effect. And in the same way, a silent mantra, or a prayer, or an expression of sheer gratefulness for life, can lead the way to becoming open to the Spirit. With a little practice, a group of online worshippers can be almost as close and welcoming a community as a group of people in a Quaker building.

Some of the customs are not the same, of course. No one stands when they speak – though it's just as important to wait a few minutes after someone else has spoken before speaking yourself. And at the end of the meeting, instead of a handshake, someone simply says 'the meeting is over', or something similar. And there may be a few notices, or perhaps everyone will be invited to go into break-out rooms for a chat. Each meeting creates its own online customs over time. No two are exactly the same.

Everyone who becomes a regular at these meetings creates their own particular approach for themselves. There are habits, just as with an in-person meeting, that need to be avoided during Quaker worship. Reading a magazine or a book, for example – other than occasional references to *Quaker faith and practice* – is one of those. Eating is another: definitely not recommended. Drinking tea, coffee or canned drinks also seems to me to be against the spirit of any religious practice. And of course, even with muted sound, talking to someone else in your household during a meeting is a clear indication that you've stopped taking part in it altogether.

Once Quaker buildings had reopened in late 2021, some groups found that an online variation, known as 'hybrid' or sometimes 'blended' meetings, can be a useful way of ensuring that Friends who aren't able to get to the meeting house can keep in touch with them. A large screen in the physical meeting room shows the online worshippers at home, who can in turn see the meeting room in one of the pictures on their screen. So the two meetings – one online and the other face-to-face – have become one.

This arrangement has proved difficult for some Quakers, while being seen as a wonderful development by others. The problem for the naysayers is that the meeting is being held in two spaces at once – a virtual space on the screen and a physical one in the room – and so the focus is split, making concentration difficult. Those who have no problem with hybrid meetings, on the other hand, are able to set aside such worries and welcome their absent friends into the meeting room without any qualms. I know one large group that has solved the problem by holding two consecutive meetings on Sunday mornings, one with a screen in the room and the other without.

Worship and Words

There are words that put people off. 'Worship' can be a tough one for some people. I've heard many say that it reminds them of church, that it sounds old-fashioned, that it's disconcerting.

'It feels like I'm supposed to be bowing down to an idol,' a woman said to me recently and I saw her point. But I did also wonder where this imaginary graven image had come from and it occurred to me that bowing down isn't necessarily such a bad thing. It depends what you're bowing down to. Personally, I can't be reminded often enough that I need to find humility in the presence of a life force I don't understand. Then again, I recall a conversation with an elderly Quaker, all his working life a peacemaker with the United Nations: 'Try thinking of yourself and God as colleagues, as partners in the same enterprise.' For him, I think, worship was a way of being in the world: it gave him the strength to hold his ground, to handle complexity, to see both sides.

The truth is that Quakers call it 'meeting for worship' because they always have; but the word now has special significance for them. In the seventeenth century, when Quakerism began, 'worship' had more of a sense of its original meaning: acknowledging the worth of something, giving 'worthship' to it. So if we take the word literally today, we go to a Quaker meeting to give 'worthship' to the divine. That seems to me to be a good definition. It certainly helps me: it encompasses my need to be humble, to give thanks, to pray. And it's a two way process – I can listen, be guided and remember that I am loved unconditionally. What's more, Quaker worship is communal: the 'worthship' reaches others. We share our blessing in a spirit of gratefulness. As we leave the meeting house, we may feel subtly changed. We may, as with my friend the peacemaker, have been given strength.

These might not be the right words for you. Your experience of Quaker worship may be entirely different. And it doesn't matter. A quotation much loved by Quakers (it is from Paul's second epistle to the Christians in Corinth) is 'The letter killeth, but the Spirit giveth life'. We shouldn't be getting hung up on an exact terminology to suit everybody, because the only relevant consideration is what happens as a result of being part of a meeting for worship. Does it help you? Is it making a difference? If, after practising it a few times, you find that it is, you'll want to be part of it for longer. If you find it that it's not beneficial, you'll understandably want to pursue your spiritual journey elsewhere.

Here's a question that strikes me as particularly unhelpful: 'Do you believe in God?' We hear it all the time, often in relation to the kind of fundamentalist atheism which takes more interest in the theory of religion than the practice of it. The implication of the enquiry is that I might be putting my trust in a fairy tale. I don't do things like that and I've never yet met a reasonable person who does. I prefer questions that are more specific, more related to personal experience. Do you encounter anything that you might call God, and if so, how? Have you experienced an overwhelming feeling of gratefulness for your existence? Do you ever have a sensation of being pushed, nudged by something outside yourself into courses of action that you might not have thought of? Do you know a happiness that comes only from the need to offer love to people?

It is the last question that seems to me to matter most. It recalls the first of the *Advices and queries*: 'Take heed, dear Friends, to the promptings of love and truth in your hearts. Trust them as the leadings of God whose Light shows us our darkness and brings us to new life.' If I listen to the promptings of love and truth in my heart, if I rely on them and allow them to dictate what I do with my life, I won't be running things on the need for greater recognition or a bigger bank balance. I'll be led by the Spirit, as Quakers often say. I'll allow myself to be guided. I'll know myself better. The result will be that what I do will become more significant, both to me and others, than what I say. 'Do you believe in God?' can easily become an invitation to talk about religious theory. It's not a question I have ever heard asked by Quakers.

'How do you encounter God?', on the other hand, is a practical query that I've known to be the starting point for countless fascinating discussions. Everyone's answer is different. Some of the most absorbing have come from those Quakers who prefer not to use the word 'God' at all. (You may recall from the Prologue that they often describe themselves as 'nontheists'.) Here is part of a piece by one such Quaker, David Boulton:

> *Nontheist Quakers use the term to include a variety of understandings, including those of atheists, humanists, agnostics, theological nonrealists, and those who experience God not as a supernatural power but as 'the ground of our being', or life itself, or nature, or the supreme symbol and imagined embodiment of our highest human values. With William Blake we want to say that, for us, God is 'mercy, pity, peace and love' in action and 'all deities reside in the human breast'.*

Speaking for myself, I have had spiritual experiences – I call them my 'hot flashes' – which convince me that something potent and elemental has become an active force in my life. I don't think they are imaginary. As a result of these encounters, I often feel drawn unavoidably towards a commitment to personal change that seems to lie beyond what I want for myself, but also fulfils me spiritually. I've found these moments difficult to predict and hard to explain. So I may perhaps be one of those who experience God as what David calls 'a supernatural power'. Yet I also find much of his description of the nontheist position to be an entirely faithful reflection of my own. It's become clear to me that differences in our perceptions of God – the Light, the Seed, the Ground Of Our Being, call it what you will – don't matter a jot if we're able to meet and 'know one another in the things that are eternal' (to quote Advice 18 of *Advices and queries*) and at the same time gain strength and impetus from the encounter. That is what happens in a Quaker meeting for worship.

David quotes Blake's 'All deities reside in the human breast'. It is a perfect paraphrase of another saying much loved by Quakers: 'that of God in everyone'. I have sometimes heard it expressed in the form of a creed, but that is not how it originally appeared. It comes from a letter written by George Fox in the late seventeenth century:

> *Be patterns, be examples in all countries, places, islands, nations, wherever you come; that your carriage and life may preach among all sorts of people, and to them. Then you will come to walk cheerfully over the world, answering that of God in every one.*

Fox takes it as read that there is that of God in us all. He suggests that the job of a faithful Quaker is to find it in other people. That means discovering love and truth in the hearts of our neighbours, colleagues, friends and, crucially, our adversaries. It means connecting with it. It can be a formidable challenge to answer that of God in people who want to do us harm, but Fox's injunction gives a practical prompt to anyone who may see it as important to try to love their enemies. He suggests that we look for, find and address the truth in the hearts of those who dislike us. Attempt to reach it. Enjoy any minuscule change it might bring. It can, after all, be a stepping stone to peace. And the impetus for this 'walking cheerfully' is the gathered meeting for worship.

'That of God in everyone' leads to another important facet of twenty-first century Quakerism: a noticeable lack of interest in talking about sin. Most Quakers of my acquaintance are clear that the doctrine of original sin – the idea that we are all born into a general condition of sinfulness that we have to lead our lives trying to expunge – is an unhelpful piece of dogma that often leads to feelings of guilt and self-hatred. Some Quakers have been inspired by the expression 'original blessing', used widely as a result of the work of the American theologian Matthew Fox, because it chimes so well with their beliefs. If we spend our lives looking for the good in people, it follows that we must believe they were born with goodness already there. Quakers don't deny that people can be corrupted. Many are convinced of the existence of evil. But they don't assume sin in others and remain convinced, as Desmond Tutu has put it, that we are 'hard-wired for goodness'.

A large number of Quakers describe themselves as Christian. *Quaker faith and practice* characterises them in a memorable phrase: 'humble learners in the school of Christ'. It is probably the case that most of these Christian Quakers don't take a literal view of certain parts of the Bible, tending to consider some of its narrative to be symbolic of the human search for God rather than actual truth. Yet, I also know Quakers for whom particular episodes – the physical resurrection of Jesus from the dead is an example – are a literal truth, a living reality on which they base their lives. And the point is that no one is arguing about it. People's beliefs are personal to them: often shared, sometimes questioned, but never decried. Quakers learn from each other.

When I first walked into a Quaker meeting, I brought with me a deep, unyielding scepticism towards the figure of Jesus. It was a reaction to a Christian upbringing that had taught me that this man was the only son of God. Yet, in the stillness of my first Quaker meeting, I felt a wound beginning to heal. Slowly, over the years, that recovery has continued and my attitudes are not the same as they were. I still fail to understand the divinity of Jesus, but I am relaxed in the company of many Quakers for whom it is a given. And I have come to accept him as a spiritual master who is part of my life. His teaching and example have helped me to know who I am. His nonviolence, in particular, has enabled me to discover a capacity to turn my back on old ways of coping with conflict. These changes have come to me in the quiet of Quaker worship. They are not the result of dogma or indoctrination, but of offering my heart and mind to God in the stillness. They have been given to me. And I am astonished to find myself acknowledging today that I am a Christian Quaker.

I've been particularly interested in talking to Quakers, some from Christian traditions and some not, who are attracted to the practices of eastern religions. Among those who come from a Buddhist tradition, I have known some who call themselves 'Buddhist Quakers', others who describe themselves as 'Quaker Buddhists' and still more who are 'Buddhists who are also Quakers'. I confess I can never quite see the distinction, but it really is up to them. It's not my place or that of any other Quaker to dispute what people hold dear when they are trying to express their most closely held convictions. As we've seen, what matters to Quakers is not what you say or think, but what you do. And I've never met one, whatever their religious background, who would want to change anything in a phrase from the Quaker peace declaration of 1660: 'The spirit of Christ, by which we are guided'. It is that spirit and that guide from which the wellspring of Quakerism derives.

So in a Quaker meeting for worship these people, with their differing experiences, traditions, backgrounds and beliefs come together in a communal practice that gives them meaning and purpose. The word 'worship' means a great deal to them, because it has acquired particular significance as a result of the transforming effect it can have on those who attend. It may not have the precise connotations it has for members of other faith traditions, but it is none the worse for that.

I'll close this section with one last definition. I find it the most resonant of all. It is found in Advice 8 of *Advices and queries*. Here it is in full.

> *Worship is our response to an awareness of God. We can worship alone, but when we join with others in expectant waiting we may discover a deeper sense of God's presence. We seek a gathered stillness in our meetings for worship so that all may feel the power of God's love drawing us together and leading us.*

I'm helped by the word 'awareness' in this context. The advice is not about 'knowledge', or 'understanding' of God. It accepts that we may only have the occasional glimpse of something outside ourselves, and it is careful not to be specific until the last sentence. There it describes with certainty the process of spiritual examination that is central to Quaker worship: seeking, being drawn together and becoming ready to be led. They are the essentials of all Quaker practice and they enable people to leave the meeting with the willingness and strength to do what love requires of them.

What Do the Children and Young People Do?

Many Quaker groups hold a children's meeting at the same time that the adults are holding theirs. Usually, everyone comes together for part of the silent worship. It's impossible to generalise about what the arrangements will be at the meeting you visit. Not all meetings have regular provision for children, so you may want to check things out first. Everything depends on the circumstances of each individual group. You can see the facilities of all the meetings in Britain by going to www.quaker.org.uk and following the 'Find a Quaker Meeting' links. It may sometimes also be a good idea to contact a meeting directly.

The nature of the activities in the children's meeting will depend on the skills and personalities of the adults who lead them, so, again, it isn't possible to be specific. It's safe to say, though, that the emphasis will always be on encouraging the participants to find their own way. Energy, creativity, talking, listening and friendliness top the list of priorities of every facilitator. Dull is not an option.

Many of the larger Quaker meetings feature a session of 'all-age worship' three or four times a year, replacing one of their regular worship sessions. These meetings are often semi-programmed – there may be songs, painting, poetry, drama – and they are planned by the adults and children together. All-age worship puts the children's contribution at the heart of the Quaker meeting. It can be a beautiful, resonant and deeply spiritual experience for everybody, regardless of their age.

If you're interested in the kinds of activity that your children may be involved in, it might be worth your while to check https://www.woodbrooke.org.uk/resource-categories/journeys-in-the-spirit/. There you will find some of the resources and advice published to help volunteers who work in children's meetings and you'll be able to gauge the tone of the work they do.

As their children get older, Quaker parents tend to leave the decisions about whether or not to attend meeting to the young people themselves. Many meetings hold sessions for people aged twelve and above, though they may not always be weekly. My own holds monthly discussion groups which are attended by young members of other local meetings and also young people who may have never been part of a Quaker group before.

Children and young people add to the rich blend of personalities and experience that characterises each Quaker community. Quakers regard everyone as of equal importance, regardless of their experience. Children and young people of every age have the same rights and opportunities. They can minister in a meeting for worship in just the same way as adults. Their voices are as valuable.

Inevitably, some find that in time their interests take them elsewhere on Sunday mornings, but that doesn't necessarily mean that they want to lose touch with Quakers. So they may want to attend one or more of the large number of activities, programmes and opportunities for friendship organised at a national or regional level for people in their teens. They don't have to be attenders of meetings to go. You will find more details at www.quaker.org.uk by searching Children and Young People.

After the Meeting

When the meeting is over, someone will deliver a few notices about future events. They may even greet you as a welcome visitor. After that, if you want to do as I did for my first tentative weeks and hurry away with your own thoughts and reflections, no one will stand in your way. If you decide to hang on a little, there will be a cup of tea or coffee, and you'll have the opportunity to chat with the people you've been worshipping with. They *are* the Quaker meeting you're visiting. Nobody leads them, no one takes decisions on their behalf, every person is of equal value. They operate without a hierarchy. The mix of personalities is different from group to group, so no two meetings are the same. Each has its own texture and identity.

It may be that you want to ask advice or check things out. If you've found the silence a struggle – not at all uncommon at a first visit – it could help to mull things over with a sympathetic and experienced Quaker: there will always be someone who is happy to talk to you. Or you might want to ask something more practical. Perhaps you have a disability and would value some help getting to the meeting house in future weeks: assistance could well be available. Or maybe you have children and want to know what arrangements are made for them. The best person to ask about those kinds of issue is the one who has just read out the notices. They will point you to the right person to talk to.

If you want to ask more general questions, don't hesitate. Quakers are there to help you. Do remember, though, that they have no creed or formal list of beliefs, so if you want to know whether Quakers believe in life after death, or if you're keen to ascertain their collective attitude to conscientious objection, you won't get an answer that speaks for the whole community. On the other hand, I'm sure you'll have a fascinating conversation. And as you continue to go back week after week, you'll begin to realise which of these Quakers are the ones who have experience and beliefs that are close to your own. And who knows, you may gradually start to align yourself with people whose views you previously discounted. Quakerism, after all, is about listening.

Most groups have discussions after meeting at least once a month. Some combine them with a visiting speaker. If you happen to arrive on one of those days, you will be welcome to stay. There is often a simple meal served on such occasions and you can be part of that too. Quakers make a point of being inclusive, and the very fact that you are with them makes you an integral part of the proceedings. You are valued. You may feel diffident, perhaps a trifle shy, and it could be that your welcomers are experiencing something similar, but you'll be seen as an essential participant for as long as you want to be.

If there's more than one Quaker meeting near your home, you may want to try out the others. I was lucky enough to live close to three other meetings when I first started and I gave each of them an experimental visit before finally ending up back where I had begun. All kinds of mundane things will contribute to your decision: the time the meeting starts, the parking, the architecture of the building, the quality of the biscuits. But the most important factor, of course, is rapport. If you find it uncomfortable to be with these people, you won't want to stay long.

The meeting where you do start to feel at home, on the other hand, is likely to become important to you. You'll enjoy the company of the people there and get to recognise their little ways. They'll look forward to greeting you. Friendships will form. And before long you'll need the answer to a common question for which I've so far only hinted at a response: 'If I want to keep coming to meetings, do I have to join the Religious Society of Friends?' Or, in other words: what's the difference between what Quakers call a 'member' and what they term an 'attender'?

As soon as you show up for the first time, you are an attender. If you keep coming, you are a regular attender and you will become a valued presence in your local meeting simply by being there. You can play a part in the meeting's affairs, you can help with the everyday work of keeping the meeting going, you can become a valued contributor to the life of this small group of people and still never join the Religious Society of Friends. If you do decide to apply for membership after a year or two, the decision will be yours alone. Your meeting will none the less be delighted and will support you in any way it can. The process of joining is simple and nurturing. I'll explain it in detail in the Epilogue.

If you join, you'll be a member not only of your meeting, but of the Religious Society of Friends as a whole. You'll be an integral part of the way Quakers in Britain are run. It's often said that Quakers have not so much abolished the priesthood as got rid of the laity. Every Quaker is a priest. Each one has a responsibility through this 'priesthood of all believers' to give energy to the work Quakers do, whether at a local or national level. For most Quakers, membership of the Society becomes a way of life. It is part of their DNA. Quakerism is not a Sunday religion. It runs right through the lives of those who practise it.

How Local Meetings are Organised

I've said that Quakers have no hierarchy and that they take decisions in a unique way that does away with majority voting, so I'm guessing that you now need the answers to some pertinent questions. How, for example, can Quakers run an organisation with no one in charge? Don't some people have to be given responsibilities? Who takes on the responsibility of handing out the responsibilities? And how can you take group decisions without listening to the will of the majority?

In this section, I'll explain a little of how a local Quaker meeting works and hope to answer all these queries in the process. It's not sensible to go into scrupulous detail: much of what goes on in a Quaker meeting is best understood by experiencing it and there is a lot that you won't need to know until you've been attending for a year or two at least. But I'll attempt to cover the ground by listing some of the most important jobs in any Quaker community and showing how vacancies are filled without requiring the services of a director of operations. I'll also explore the unique method by which Quakers take their policy decisions.

The 'meeting for worship for business' lies at the heart of the Quaker way and is explained in full in its own section a little later. For the moment, it's enough to say that Quakers' search for the divine is as much a part of their decision making as it is of their regular worship. Business meetings, which are often now held online, are based on silence and stillness. The participants put prejudgements out of their minds and allow themselves to be guided by the Spirit. Nobody tries to prove anything. As the meeting gathers, they find a collective way forward, rather than arguing points or taking sides.

Because of its spiritual dimension, the outcome of a Quaker business meeting may prove to be entirely different from what might reasonably have been expected at the beginning.

In British meetings there is no pastor and, except in the very largest groups, no administrative officer, so when there are tasks to be fulfilled, members of the meeting who feel able to help are asked to take them on. Ambition has no part to play. When people are invited to carry out a role in the meeting, they are being requested to give thoughtful service, not further a Quaker career. Some of the duties carry a heavy time commitment or a high level of responsibility, often both: they are normally done by experienced members of the Society. Many other roles are less onerous.

Quaker meetings need to bring in a small income in order to survive: it normally comes from a combination of money earned from the letting of their building, if they have one, and financial contributions from their members and attenders. So, one or two people from each meeting are appointed to be treasurers. As we've seen, many groups set up a children and young people's committee. There may also be a library committee and an outreach group. And every meeting needs people to publish the newsletter, make the coffee and do the other numerous roles that help any organisation to tick along from week to week.

The length of each appointment is fixed, and people are given a clear date when it will end. Usually, it's suggested that a person takes on a role for three years at a time and then stops. Two consecutive three year terms in any given capacity are generally considered to be the absolute maximum. After that, they are asked to 'lay down their service', a Quaker expression implying a careful, unselfish release from a valued contribution. Frequently, they consider taking on another responsibility instead, but they don't continue in the area they have become used to.

This is a good way of ensuring that a person gives service, rather than hanging on for dear life to a particular area of expertise. We are all familiar with the scenario in which someone continues to fulfil a function on behalf of a community because they turn out to be good at it. In a short time, it becomes natural for them to regard themselves as indispensable and, who knows, others may begin to agree. Before long, everyone thinks they are uniquely gifted and they end up staying for years. Not only that, but a hierarchy has developed, because other people defer to them. Quakers find this problematical and take pains to ensure it doesn't happen. Members of the Society undertake roles, sometimes involving qualities of leadership, often bearing great responsibility, always entailing hard work and a deep understanding of the task. And then, after three or sometimes six years, they move on and do something else. They are happy to do it because they understand that they are giving service, not promoting their own interests.

Visitors and new attenders are not requested to do jobs, so don't worry that you'll be pounced on: no one takes on anything until they are ready for it. After a few months or years of attending the meeting, you may be asked to try a light task, perhaps coordinating the leaflets in the entrance hall or helping with the refreshments, to find out how you take to it. If it's the wrong time for you or you don't yet feel committed enough to Quakers, you only have to say so – though you may think it's worth taking the approach seriously, since it was made after careful consideration.

So now we come to the important question: if there's no

hierarchy, who gives out these jobs? The answer is that the whole community does it, by holding a business meeting during which they appoint a small group called a nominations committee, who are asked to make recommendations. The committee meets regularly and looks at the various three-year terms that may be drawing to a close, thinking of new people who could be prepared to take on the work. This is a prayerful process, in which the names of possible candidates can arise unexpectedly and without planning. Members of the committee go on to have conversations with the people who are being suggested, so that they can discuss the implications of taking on the job.

Often, the role put forward to a person is the last one they might have envisaged for themselves. But they take the proposition seriously, because it arose in a meeting for worship and as a result it has the ring of truth about it. So Quakers become used to what they call 'the tap on the shoulder': being asked to take on an appointment that they aren't sure they can do and saying yes to it anyway. It is part of living adventurously.

When the nominations committee has assembled a list of candidates for the roles that need to be filled, they come back to the whole group in a meeting for worship for business. Each name is carefully considered. If the members of that meeting agree to the nominations, they appoint the people to their new roles, letting them know that the job is theirs for the next three years. After which time, of course, they will be asked to stop.

It is not democracy. Yet everybody is part of it, and – since it all happens during gathered meetings for worship for business – it is a process that results in unexpected affirmations and unlooked-for outcomes. Quakers get used to it. It is part of being open to the Spirit.

Three Key Roles

Most nominations committees have a considerable number of appointments to make. There are inevitably fewer opportunities for service in small meetings than large ones, but some key roles are essential in all of them. One, as we've seen, is that of treasurer, a job which is the same as it would be in any organisation. Another is convenor of the premises committee, the body in charge of the upkeep of the meeting house, assuming there is one. And there are a further three without which a Quaker meeting cannot function successfully: the clerk, the pastoral Friends and the elders. And, since they are not common in non-Quaker groups, I'll spend the next few paragraphs explaining each of them briefly in turn.

All Quaker bodies, from the smallest committee to a thousand-strong annual gathering, have a clerk. If you've ever attended a meeting for worship, the chances are that you'll have seen the clerk at work. The local meeting's clerk is the human channel through whom all the administrative work flows. Some meetings have one or two assistant clerks who help to share the responsibility, but it's often a solo job, so I'll assume for our purposes that we are only talking about one.

The clerk is often the person who reads out the notices at the end of the meeting, so newcomers sometimes think understandably that they are some kind of figurehead. You know enough about Quakers by now to realise that isn't so. Certainly, for the three years the clerk is in the post, their personality becomes well known to everyone: letters are addressed to the clerk and often read out; the clerk will almost certainly be the person announcing births, marriages and deaths; it's part of the clerk's job to answer enquiries from the public; and so on. The clerk also has responsibilities within the meeting for worship for business, which you can read about in the next section. But no one is in charge, of course, so the clerk is simply giving service, carrying out decisions made by the group as a whole.

Every month or two, there is a meeting for worship for business: it's hoped that everyone who is a member will attend if they can. Those who have yet to join are also welcome, so long as they have first checked it out with the clerk. The clerk's role is to draw up the agenda, listen, discern a possible outcome and write the minute. Groups and individuals may report to this wider body and bring their issues, plans and questions to it. So Premises Committee may ask the opinion of the meeting on a specific piece of renovation work that needs to be done; or Outreach Committee may request money for a public event. And, as with any meeting for worship, the procedure is subject to the welcome reversals and happy surprises that bubble up when any group of people open themselves to the leadings of the Spirit.

Pastoral Friends – known in some meetings as the pastoral support team – are the people responsible for the care of everyone at the local meeting. For example, it will be a pastoral Friend you will get in touch with if your disability makes it difficult to get to meeting by public transport, or if you're thinking of joining the Religious Society of Friends. Pastoral Friends send birthday cards to the meeting's children, support members and attenders who are ill and do all they can to ensure that visitors are well looked after. When conflicts arise, it is the job of pastoral Friends to work privately with the people involved to help them to find an understanding. They ensure that people working away from their local area know they are not forgotten. They keep in touch with the parents of newborn children.

Most but not all meetings assign a small number of their regulars to a specific pastoral Friend. This way, you get to know the person whose job it is to be available to you in times of need. If my friend in group therapy – the one who saw meeting for worship as a place to unburden himself – had known who his pastoral Friend was, he might have found help more quickly.

'Elder' is a word first coined by members of the early Christian churches. It has been commandeered by many Protestant groups since, so it may come with unwelcome associations for you, depending on your background. Some Quakers are less than happy with the word, which leads to the elders being known variously as 'the spiritual nurture team' or 'the eldership team' in some meetings. At the time I am writing this, 'elder' seems to be the one used most often, but I won't be surprised if that changes in due course.

Elders can be of any age – I know one in his twenties – and they are almost always members of the Religious Society of Friends. Their job is to look after the spiritual life of the meeting, particularly supporting the right holding of worship. Inevitably, much of their work overlaps with that of pastoral Friends. One or two brief examples: both groups work together to ensure that regulars of the meeting who are ill get a meeting for worship in their homes; they help to arrange funerals with the families of those who have died; and they give help and support to people who are considering joining the Religious Society of Friends.

They are most visible to you in the meeting room as the Quakers who shake hands first at the end of a meeting for worship. If you're new, it may be a good idea to find out who the elders are: there may well be more than one or two and they can often be the best people to talk to if you are encountering difficulties in meeting. Perhaps it's hard for you to centre down? Or maybe you thought a particular piece of ministry was baffling or inappropriate? The elders should be able to offer useful advice.

And they may agree with you, of course. When I'd been going to Quaker meetings for about six months, I heard a piece of ministry that struck me as inappropriate. A man stood up in the stillness and broke the silence. 'Apropos of nothing at all ... ' he began, and continued to talk about, well, nothing at all, for five minutes and more. He told us a joke he had heard last week and a jovial item on a radio programme from the day before. Nothing connected. I found it difficult to reconcile this with anything I'd read or heard about Quaker meetings and I failed to understand what I was supposed to do with it. How on earth could I incorporate it into my worship? I felt strangely hurt. So afterwards I found an elder and spoke to her. She said that she was as dismayed as I was and that, to my surprised delight, she was going to do something about it.

It was only then that I discovered another of the responsibilities of an elder. If a meeting is disturbed by someone ministering or behaving unhelpfully, it is the elder's duty to speak about it kindly and in love. It can be done during the meeting for worship by standing and saying what needs to be said ('our Friend has given us a lot to think about...'), or it may be delayed until a suitable time afterwards, when the elder can have a quiet conversation with the person. It is not a rebuke and still less a punishment. But sometimes the job of ensuring that the meeting's worship is held properly requires a little plain speaking.

Meeting for Worship for Business

Quakers hold their business meetings in an unusual way. People call it the Quaker Business Method, but that implies a formula. It leaves out the essential and unpredictable element of the process, the aspect that makes it work, which is that Quaker business is undertaken in the context of a meeting for worship. In essence it is held, either face-to-face or online, in exactly the same way as a normal silent meeting.

One person will have been appointed to be the clerk (see Three Key Roles). It is a role rather like a combination of chair and secretary in a regular business setting: the clerk prepares the agenda and writes down the minutes, reflecting what has been agreed. There, however, the comparisons stop, because the detail of how the clerk goes about the task is different.

The meeting begins with a short period, perhaps ten minutes, of silent worship. The clerk explains the first item on the agenda and waits for spoken contributions, usually with the words, 'The matter is before you, Friends.' The job of the participants is to abandon any preconceived notions and to listen not just to each other, but crucially to the promptings of love and truth, to the leadings of God, in their hearts. The job of the clerk is to listen for the working of the Spirit as it is manifested in the meeting.

Members of the group who have something to say stand one by one and, in the stillness, express their thoughts on the subject in hand. There is a short period of silence between contributions as the meeting reflects on what has been put forward. It may be that individuals begin to change their stance as a result, but no one uses rhetoric in an attempt to convince. What is spoken is ministry. This, I repeat, is a meeting for worship.

The clerk may take notes, but what they are really listening for is a unity, a oneness, in what is offered by members of the meeting, because there will be no votes. The job of the clerk is to discern the sense of the meeting and only move to the next stage when they are sure that unity has been reached. Often, a period of silence may be a factor in helping the clerk to understand that the last spoken ministry has become the feeling of everybody present.

That feeling may not necessarily reflect what we might call 'agreement'. What frequently happens in the Quaker silence is that participants who are not of the same mind none the less recognise clearly what must be done. So what they have established in their decision is unity, as distinct from unanimity. And anyway, whose decision is it? Some would say that in the silence they are seeking the will of God. If that's right, their job is not to bandy opinions, but to unearth an outcome that has to happen. Decisions taken in a Quaker business meeting can be touched by a divine alchemy that is easier to experience than it is to explain.

When the meeting has achieved a way forward, the clerk writes a minute of what they believe to be the feeling of those present. If the matter is complex this may take some time. The group waits in the stillness of worship while the minute is being written (this is called 'upholding the clerk') and when it is complete, the clerk reads it out. At this stage, members of the meeting suggest amendments and the clerk notes them. The meeting and the minute must reflect each other accurately before everyone moves to the next agenda item. Very occasionally, a decision can't be reached and the matter is held over to another meeting. However, Quakers are aware that this can be a lazy option and avoid it if they can.

The result is often described as 'consensus', but I think

that's a careless word to use. Consensus is secular. It implies general accord and, as we have seen, that may not necessarily be the outcome of a successful Quaker business meeting. Nor can this be called 'majority rule': no one takes sides, no one can bully, they simply make decisions together and remain loyal to them. Seen purely as a business method, it is often thought to be slow, but it is, by the same token, also thorough and inclusive. And because the minutes are read out carefully at the time, they can't be changed afterwards. What is decided has been decided: it is there in black and white, agreed by everyone present.

The responsibility borne by the clerk is considerable, but when the job is done well it transforms the proceedings. A good clerk can tell when members of the meeting are in unity long before they know it themselves. An experienced clerk may call for a period of silence when Quakers are in conflicted positions, knowing that it can allow them the space they need for prayer and reflection. A sensitive clerk remembers that this is not a talking shop but a spirit-led meeting for worship and understands that, because of its religious weight, a gathered meeting can deliver unexpected and revelatory outcomes. One person's quiet observation can imperceptibly become the intention of everyone.

I have asked two friends for a little of their experience of Quaker business meetings.

I recall a powerful example of a meeting reaching unity on a controversial matter. When the question came before us, half who spoke were in favour and half against. The clerk suggested an extended period of silence. When people spoke again, a few had changed their views but we were still deeply divided. Again we sat in silence. A Friend rose.

He said, 'It is now clear to me that we should do what is proposed'. And sat down. It had been said many times before in similar words, but this time nobody else stood up to speak. In due course the clerk presented a minute. What had changed? Only the perception of us all in the silence that the decision was right at that time, however strongly many of us might have felt to the contrary. We were in unity.

I remember a time when a matter was presented to the meeting and I had an immediate sense that the action proposed was wrong. I was gratified when others stood to say they found it unacceptable and after a short while the clerk prepared to write a minute. Then one person rose and spoke with thoughtful, stumbling words, to suggest that the proposed action was one that we were being invited to take in a spirit of openness and inclusiveness; and one that could enrich our community if we embraced it. The silence deepened. Words were voiced: 'I hope that we can accept this proposal.' There was a clear sense that we had been taken up by the scruff of our necks and put down in a different place from our sensible selves. And the outcome felt right.

These stories are good examples of the kind of unexpected realisations that can take place in a gathered meeting for worship for business. I hope you experience them one day, face-to-face or online, even if other aspects of the Quaker path prove not to be for you. Each has its own particular beauty.

The Wider Quaker Community

Quakers in Britain are a bottom-up, not a top-down organisation. In other words, the people who initiate action are individuals and committees at local level. They bring their ideas, suggestions and worries to their meeting for worship for business. If that meeting decides that a matter is of wider importance to the Quaker community, it is brought to the attention of their area meeting.

Area meetings are clusters of local meetings, usually between five and ten in each, who meet together regularly to discuss their business and any other matters they may need to share. They don't have separate buildings of their own, preferring to hold their events in one or other of their meeting places. As their name implies, geography is what links them to each other, but like local meetings, each celebrates rich and lasting personal friendships and a strong sense of community. Area meetings are a source of cohesion among Quakers, offering mutual support and accountability, enabling a local meeting of, say, ten people to be as resonant as one of two hundred.

For these reasons, people who become members of the Religious Society of Friends in Britain join their area meeting, rather than the smaller local meeting where they actually worship. Area meetings receive money from local meetings, and it is pooled so that they are able, for instance, to send members and attenders on weekend courses they might not otherwise be able to afford. They also appoint the elders, the pastoral Friends, and the Quakers whose responsibility it is to look after property. They act as facilitators and co-ordinators, ensuring that all the Quakers in the area, including children and young people, have opportunities for fellowship, spiritual development and pastoral care.

They also support them in their 'concerns' – a word they use to describe Quakers' spiritual prompts to take action in the world – ensuring that, whenever appropriate, important matters are raised at meetings that involve the entire community of Quakers, country-wide. These have been a regular feature of Quaker life since 1668 and are held once a year. For most of that time, and for obvious reasons, they have been known as Yearly Meetings.

Yearly Meetings bring together Quakers from all the area meetings in Britain. The sessions are held in the same way as local business meetings and in the same spirit of gathered worship, the only difference being that they consist of a larger number of people. It is an education to attend one, to see Quaker business working at its best with hundreds of participants and no rhetoric. The sessions are, for obvious reasons, normally restricted to members of the Religious Society of Friends, but if you have a word with an elder or the clerk of your meeting, they can ensure that you are able to attend. If you find you are interested in Quakerism, I recommend that you try to get to one. Two notable sessions worth highlighting have been the one in 1994, at which the entire text of *Quaker faith and practice* was approved section by section by over a thousand people in a meeting for worship; and another in 2009, when a similar number agreed to express support for same sex marriages and to lobby government for changes in the law.

Recent Yearly Meetings have been held as hybrid meetings in the way that I've already described in the Meeting for Worship for Business section. A large screen showing the faces of Quakers who can't make it in person joins the numbers in the meeting hall, making the gatherings the largest that British Quakers have ever held. At the meeting held in the summer of 2024, over two thousand people of all ages attended in person and online, all equally involved and all equally able to contribute.

The ease with which British Quakers have taken to video conferencing has also made it possible to make changes to the frequency of these Yearly Meetings. At the 2024 gathering Quakers decided to hold them four times a year, starting in 2027 – not four Yearly Meetings, which would seem more than a little eccentric, but one continuous Yearly Meeting held in four stages. This was an imaginative move, making Quaker decision-making more transparent and interactive. To quote the closing statement from the gathering in 2024: 'There are no observers in Quakers; we are all participants.'

These meetings are the voice of Britain Yearly Meeting, which is – somewhat confusingly – the name given to the whole British organisation of Quakers. In the same way that your neighbourhood Quaker meeting *is* the Quakers who make it up, Britain Yearly Meeting *is* all the Quakers in Britain. It is known colloquially as BYM and represents the Society's ultimate authority. It runs the building I first entered, Friends House, and employs the people whose work is based there. It is the channel through which Quaker policy is decided and expressed.

Everyday Blessing

When Robert Barclay, a seventeenth century theologian, described his first Quaker encounter, he said 'I found the evil weakening in me, and the good raised up'. It is possibly the first description in print of a gathered meeting and tells a familiar story reflected in the experience of many first-timers since. After a few visits, they discover that the silence gets easier, the stillness more agreeable. When they start to be familiar with the practice, it seems natural to lapse into silence in the way that Quakers often do before discussions, as a prelude to meals, at the close of business. Quiet and stillness have become an everyday blessing.

Gathered worship is the way Quakers do things. If I have a moral dilemma – perhaps I feel torn by conflicting loyalties, or maybe I'm not sure whether I should move to another area or accept a job offer – I can request what Quakers call a 'meeting for clearness'. This may take a number of forms, but is essentially a discussion between me and some selected friends to help me come to a decision. Notes are often taken, but there's no clerk and no formal minute. Meetings for clearness may be held when someone is thinking of joining the Society. They are frequently used when Quakers find themselves in conflict. Couples who are considering marriage or civil partnership sometimes find them a help in reaching their decision together. Gathered worship can be a tool for reaching understanding and helping change.

Quaker weddings are often beautiful events and they too are meetings for worship. The guests are welcomed by an elder who explains the Quaker way – for many, this may be their first experience of it – and the room slowly fills with the deep, familiar silence. When they feel ready, the people who are marrying stand and, using a specifically Quaker form of words ('Friends, I take this my friend...'), they make their declarations. The meeting falls into silence again. During the stillness, guests may minister in loving support. As the proceedings draw to a close, each person who was present when the pair first spoke signs a certificate proclaiming the marriage they have witnessed and recording the pledge that was made. Every name is there: men, women, children, babies, all play a part in the finished document, which becomes one of the couple's most treasured possessions, along with the legal document that they sign afterwards.

Quaker funerals and memorial meetings (often called meetings of 'thanksgiving for the grace of God as shown in the life' of the person who has died) are frequently happy and fulfilling occasions, held in the silence of worship. They usually take place in crematoriums or local meeting houses; sometimes both – first one and then the other. They tend to be as much Quaker as family affairs: indeed, I've attended some which have been bursting with people jammed into corners, sitting on the floor between the seats, perched on window sills, all expressing through the stillness of a Quaker meeting their feelings for someone who has been dear to them. Spontaneous ministry, spoken or sung by friends, gradually bestows on the occasion a unique form, shape and character. The unvarnished nature of Quaker worship gives everyone the space to respond to the promptings of love and truth in their hearts.

In *Quaker faith and practice*, there is a chapter entitled 'Varieties of Religious Service'. Newcomers might expect to pick it up and find details there of further forms of corporate worship. A baptism maybe? Or a Quaker version of the eucharist? If they do, they won't get far, because that's not what Quakers mean by 'service'. Instead, the chapter is about obeying the promptings of the Spirit, giving service as a religious person to the world at large: prison visiting perhaps, or being a college chaplain. Quakers sometimes call this work their 'faith in action', and you can read more about it in Part Three. Services, as held in churches, both Christian and not, have never been part of the Quaker way.

Quaker parents don't hold naming ceremonies: mother and father simply bring their newborn to the meeting house, where the assembled company welcomes the baby with enthusiasm and joy. Nor do they take part in religious practices in which people make promises on behalf of their children. They don't vow to bring them up in a particular way. Indeed, Quakers never swear oaths of any kind, because to do so implies for them a double standard: 'I'm not lying now, because I'm under oath, but it was different yesterday and I might have second thoughts tomorrow.' So Quakers have no truck with the idea of swearing to be truthful: in courts of law they 'affirm', an alternative that was initiated in the eighteenth century specifically to help them and other religious groups who felt the same way.

Quakers' commitment to truth and integrity is a consequence of their religious lives, not an aspiration. It's part of what they call 'sacramental living'. I'll have more to say about this, but it's worth mentioning now in order to understand why Quakers do not take part in a communion service, eucharist or mass. I've known visitors from Christian backgrounds to find this shocking, even irreligious. For them, the allegory implicit in the rituals of the sacraments has become a living reality. While Quakers have no desire to deny them their beliefs, they do not share a love of symbol. Quakers believe in an unmediated relationship with God and they hold that the sacred is to be found in the everyday. If all of life is holy, we do not need to sanctify it. What we can choose instead is to live sacramentally.

A sacrament, the dictionary tells us, is 'a religious act which is seen as an outward and visible sign of inward and spiritual grace'. The Quaker response is to say yes – and not to stop there. Why not make living itself the religious act? Why not do everything in that same sacramental spirit? Why not seek and find that of God in everyone? Religious people are sometimes thought to be 'holier than thou' – Quakers say that we are all as holy as one other. Back at the beginning of Part One, I remarked that there is no difference between the sacred and the secular. If that's not to be just a well-meaning sound bite, it changes everything: how we live, what we do and why we do it. And it has been the Quaker way for over three hundred and seventy years.

Part Two

We ... live in expectation of encounter, transformation and action in the world. This is what means to be a Quaker, and we can see it reflected in the stories from our past that we choose to remember and reprint.

Ben Pink Dandelion, 2015

Picking up the Threads

Context is a character in every story. Quakers of the 1650s – sure, uncompromising, black-hatted – seem light years away from the free-thinking folk who inhabit meeting houses today. In the same way, those who lived a hundred years later, familiar in the person of the caricatured wag who beams out from oatmeal packets, bear no apparent relation to anything we might want to emulate in the twenty-first century. And images of Elizabeth Fry and Joseph Rowntree, celebrated figures of the eighteen and nineteen hundreds, give us little to go on if we want to know what it's like to be a Quaker now.

So where are the connections? How did Quakers get here from there? In this section, I hope to hint at some answers. I'm not attempting to give you a history of Quakerism: that's done well in a number of books I'll recommend later. Nor am I suggesting that you have to know anything of the evolution of Quakers if you decide to be part of their meetings. I'm simply attempting to put a little of their centuries-old experience into context and give you something to go on. If it's of no interest to you at the moment, I hope you'll jump straight to Part Three.

Beginnings

Let's begin with a small, local event which happened over three and a half centuries ago. It still resonates with Quakers today.

In 1652, a man rose to his feet during a church service in Ulverston in Lancashire (now Cumbria), and stood on the bench. He was strongly built and a formidable speaker. He addressed the preacher. 'You will say Christ saith this,' he said to the man in the pulpit, 'and the apostles say this; but *what canst thou say?* Art thou a child of Light and hast walked in the Light, and what thou speakest is it inwardly from God?' It must have been a heart-stopping moment: on one side a priest, comfortably quoting the words of Jesus, evoking the apostles, doing what he had always done, and on the other a tender man, but also a rabble-rouser, explaining why it just wasn't enough. 'Never mind what you can quote, tell us your experience. What can you *say*? And does it come from that of God within you?' Writing the story down forty years later, a woman in the congregation recalled her reaction: 'I saw clearly we were all wrong ... We are all thieves. We have taken the scriptures in words and know nothing of them in ourselves ... I saw it was the truth and I could not deny it.'

The man was George Fox and the woman Margaret Fell. Both were to play a big part in the development of Quakerism during its formative years. Their partnership – they were married seventeen years later – was crucial in setting up

Quakers as a coherent religious organisation. Fox is often named as the founder of Quakerism and 1652 as the year of its inception, but neither is strictly true. From the start, it was a popular, grassroots movement. It developed gradually in the 1640s in the thick of England's tumultuous civil war, probably through some of the many small sects that sprang up in that decade – there were Ranters, Diggers and Seekers ('seeker' is still used by Quakers to describe anyone whose spiritual journey is alive and continuing) – and by 1650 it was already a force to be reckoned with. Quakers had fine speakers, among them James Nayler, Edward Burrough, Richard Farnsworth and William Dewsbury. The first two, Nayler and Burrough, were often considered to be the main spokespeople during Quakerism's earliest days, but in the first years of the new decade, the 1650s, George Fox began to emerge as a charismatic leader. Quakers being Quakers, this leader was part of a team.

In 1652, Fox was twenty-eight, a thinker of profound seriousness and a born communicator. His education had been scant, but his understanding of religion and biblical history was prodigious. He was rough and uncultured, with an extraordinary magnetism. And he spoke simply. He said that no amount of education, university degrees or understanding of theology can turn someone into a priest: only God can do that. He ridiculed the clergy, calling their churches 'steeple houses', because God does not dwell in temples. And he believed – no, he *knew* – that each of us can have a direct relationship with the divine without the mediation of another person. 'Your teacher is within you,' he wrote, 'look not forth.'

In his journal, he described a spiritual experience that he had had as a young man. 'When all my hopes [in priests and preachers] and in all men were gone,' he wrote, 'so that I had nothing outwardly to help me ... then, oh then, I heard a voice which said, "There is one, even Christ Jesus, that can speak to thy condition", and when I heard it my heart did leap for joy.' He said that he discovered this *experimentally* – or in modern English, *by experience*. Fox's message was that we all need Jesus and we have only to look inside ourselves to find him. He talked often of 'the Christ within'. He said that what people called 'the second coming' of the Messiah was indeed at hand, but that it was going to happen inside each of us, if we let it.

'Speak to thy condition' is a quotation which often comes up when Quakers talk today. 'I must do that,' they say, 'because it speaks to my condition.' When I first heard it, it struck me as self-conscious, given that this was supposed to be a conversation in modern English. But I now see it as unimprovable as an expression of the spiritual inspiration at the heart of Quaker faith. It acknowledges the spiritual hole, the hunger for truth that has to be satisfied in us. It accepts that we must be ready psychologically before we can come to terms with the prospect of a new challenge. And it recognises that we can only grasp the workings of the spirit by experiencing them. 'This speaks to my condition' are five crisp words defining a spark that has fired the life and work of thousands of Quakers since George Fox began his journey.

In 1652, Fox climbed a hillside, Pendle Hill in Lancashire, and underwent another spiritual awakening. It came upon him that there was, as he put it, 'a great people to be gathered' and he accepted the task of doing the gathering. His mission was to tell the whole world that the religious environment in which they were living was passive, misguided and wrong; that everyone should wake up to that of God within them; that each person, whatever their education, could be a priest in the eyes of God. Until Fox's moment on Pendle Hill, Quakers had been content to preach at a local, personal level: as he looked down on the towns and villages below, he realised that his campaign had to grow in ambition. It needed to reach out to people everywhere, to the nobility, to government, to kings, to popes. So in 1654, a group of around seventy young Quaker evangelists began to spread around the country, holding public meetings in town centres and on village greens, preaching repentance and transformational change.

They called themselves Friends of Truth. Truth for them meant more than just authenticity, integrity, or an absence of lying. It went deeper, to the very core of things: Truth with a capital 'T' acquired new meaning, expressing not only the word of God, but the godliness in each of us. Friends of Truth spoke of the Seed, of the Christ within people: women as well as men. They preached equality in the spirit. Margaret Fell wrote a pamphlet called *Women's Speaking Justified*, arguing that women could be ministers. This was revolutionary stuff: it flew in the face of all accepted religious norms. Personal experience was now being put above the teaching of the church, above the words of the clergy, above even the Bible.

Friends of Truth rejected double standards. They refused to take oaths, quoting Matthew's gospel ('swear not at all') and they also, crucially, withheld the payment of tithes – money and goods demanded by the church to maintain its clergy and buildings – believing them to be unjust, inequitable and immoral. (The Quaker Edward Burrough calculated at the time that the church was exacting around £1,500,000 a year in tithes, an eye-watering sum by any standards.) So the Friends of Truth persuaded thousands of people to withdraw their support, and in the process alienated the authorities both of church and state.

They extended their passion for spiritual equality to the details of everyday living, showing aggressive disregard for the niceties of seventeenth century etiquette. They refused to remove their hats to social superiors and never bowed to them. They were contemptuous of social status and called everybody 'thou' and 'thee', ignoring the more respectful 'you', which was how everyone else was saying it. Frippery and frills were out: they dressed plainly in sober colours, carefully avoiding the use of unnecessary fabric. Hardly surprisingly, as a result of their speech, clothes and black hats, they were recognised as Quakers from twenty paces. People got used to spotting them as cranks and troublemakers.

Violence and controversy followed them wherever they went. They produced endless pamphlets expressing their passionately held religious views, each matched by more literature from their opponents explaining just how misguided and wrong-headed these heretics were. No sooner did they rise to speak in public than they were knocked down, roughed up or done over. On one occasion, after George Fox had spoken in a church, the congregation beat him up with their Bibles. Thousands of Quakers were imprisoned. Fox himself was arrested and jailed for blasphemy many times, but always held firm. When George thought something, it was settled. He once wrote on a cell wall, 'I was never in prison that it was not the means of bringing multitudes out of their prisons'.

Britain in the seventeenth century was a restless and explosive place. Random incarcerations and street violence were accepted means of solving problems and, in a way that seems unimaginable now, everyone was interested in religion. It was a hot topic. Change was in the air and Quakers converted huge numbers of people to their way of life. They held impromptu free-for-alls in which speakers energised and infuriated noisy crowds. Anyone in the audience who seemed interested in the ways of Quakers was spotted and quietly led off to take part in a silent meeting there and then. The stillness of the worship captivated newcomers: they were hooked.

Many of the converts were members of the gentry, sometimes even the aristocracy: Quakerism was no respecter of class. And as a result, Quakers acquired some accomplished writers – never a bad thing when you have a cause to promote – two of whom in particular stand out as being of interest to us. The first was William Penn, the son of an admiral, who was converted to Quakerism at the age of twenty-two and consequently thrown out of the house by his father. Penn became a good friend to George Fox and wrote a number of Quaker classics, including *No Cross No Crown* and *Primitive Christianity Revived*, a title which says much about how Quakers saw their new religious faith.

The other early convert who is still widely read by Quakers was Isaac Penington. He and his wife Mary were sceptical of the new movement at the beginning, but found themselves slowly captivated by the truthfulness and clarity they found there. Isaac went on to write vast quantities of pamphlets, letters and books. Many of them are a little chewy for modern tastes, but others contain passages which speak in ringing tones to readers today. Here is a quotation from a letter he wrote in Aylesbury Gaol:

> *Our life is love, and peace, and tenderness; and bearing one with another, and forgiving one another, and not laying accusations one against another; but praying for one another, and helping one another up with a tender hand.*

That short paragraph says a lot about those Quakers. It came out of a prison cell in which the writer was experiencing hideous degradation, yet it shows an ability to find meaning, to encounter God, not only in others but in the mental torture of an impossible predicament. It gives an insight into the loving kindness and compassion that bound together the early Quaker communities. And, perhaps above all, it seems to me to encapsulate in a few lines the rejection of egotism, the abandonment of self-interest, which was and remains a key factor in the lives of Quakers.

None the less, you may notice a paradox here – and, if you do, there are a lot of twenty-first century Quakers who notice it with you. If this new religious faith was about the relinquishment of self, how come its proponents stood on street corners proclaiming the absolute rightness of their cause? Shouldn't their private humility have been reflected in their public behaviour? Fair points, both of them: it would certainly be unusual today to encounter a Quaker telling the world to repent. Yet, putting their behaviour into context, I can see good reasons for the ways of the pioneers. They identified a problem that they regarded as a spiritual emergency and they treated it as such. It became natural for them to tell everyone that that there was another path, that they could trust their own experience, that they didn't need to go looking for God, because God wasn't lost. And they did it in the way they knew, in the style of the times, by preaching and proclaiming.

Nowhere is the paradox more clearly seen than in the life and personality of George Fox. In his writings, we meet a man who seems almost impossibly intemperate and pig-headed and entirely different from any other Quaker who ever lived. He flayed audiences with his tongue. And his message, always passionate, often sounds furiously self-righteous. He is still remembered in Staffordshire as the man who walked into Lichfield on market day and badmouthed the entire population with one memorable phrase ('Woe to the bloody city of Lichfield!') and it's impossible to read his journal for long without coming across a description of someone as 'full of filth' or 'an enemy to Truth'.

Yet, this is also the person responsible for some of the most quietly inspiring words in all Quaker literature. He is the man who envisaged 'an ocean of darkness and death, but an infinite ocean of light and love, which flowed over the ocean of darkness', who encouraged us to 'owe to no man anything but love' and who suggested that 'Truth doth flourish, as the rose and lilies do grow among the thorns and the plants atop the hills, and upon them the lambs doth skip and play'. He also seems to have been partly responsible for a brilliantly written declaration of peace and nonviolence made to Charles II in 1660. It reads today as powerfully as ever. A short extract gives a little of its flavour:

> *All bloody principles and practices we do utterly deny, with all outward wars, and strife, and fightings with outward weapons, for any end, or under any pretence whatsoever, and this is our testimony to the whole world.*

For all Fox's vocal hostility to everyone he disagreed with, his diaries are remarkable for their commitment to nonviolence. He was beaten, bruised and bloodied, but not once did he fight back. He seems at heart to have been a gentle person. After his death, William Penn wrote an appreciation of George's life. He described him as 'of an innocent life, no busy-body, nor self-seeker, neither touchy nor critical: what fell from him was very inoffensive, if not very edifying. So meek, contented, modest, easy, steady, tender, it was a pleasure to be in his company.'

Perhaps we can have it both ways. Fox certainly experienced mood swings and it has been suggested that he may have suffered from bipolar disorder. He was a visionary. And his wisdom and energy for life were combined with a deep understanding of human psychology. There is a touching story of him told years after his death in a biography of William Penn. William, being an aristocrat as well as a Quaker, found it quite a problem to give up his expensive clothes. In particular, he had difficulty abandoning the sword that clung habitually to his side. It was a weapon that had once saved his life and he was unwilling to get rid of it, but he knew that Quakers would expect it of him. So he asked George Fox's advice. 'Wear your sword as long as you can,' Fox suggested. Not long afterwards, they met again and Penn's sword was not hanging from his belt. 'William, where's your sword?' asked Fox. 'I took your advice,' said Penn, 'and wore it as long as I could.'

'Wear it as long as you can' is advice still offered by Quakers. Old ways are hard to give up, but if we accept the difficulty and live with it, we discover – sometimes after many years – an ability to move on. We incorporate the change by finding it increasingly impossible to live in any other way. In my experience, this can apply to religion itself. Sudden conversions can be troublesome and frightening. Yet by 'wearing' a former, much loved religious practice as long as we can, we give it the respect it needs before discovering, little by little, the capacity to let it go.

William Penn didn't take long to announce his Quakerism and when he did, he went at it full-tilt. Within a year he had written a pamphlet called *Truth Exalted* (described by Samuel Pepys as 'a ridiculous, nonsensical book'), in which he condemned every religion except the one he had just made his own. That is often an unfortunate trait in converts, but in Penn's case it was short-lived. He soon emerged as a uniquely tolerant and forgiving man. Within ten years he proposed an ingenious scheme to buy up vast areas of land in America, so that Quakers could emigrate to safety. And it happened. He bought the whole of East Jersey, then West Jersey and in the early 1680s he was given another huge tract of American land by the king, in settlement of a debt owed to Penn's father. He started a Quaker settlement there, eventually named Pennsylvania. His new community became a refuge for persecuted minorities of many different faiths who were allowed to worship freely. This was called his 'holy experiment'. And it became the starting point of the Quaker movement in America, where it has continued to prosper ever since.

In 1689 the Act of Toleration in Britain allowed freedom of worship to nonconformist groups and effectively put the persecution of Quakers to an end. They enjoyed the peace that was offered to them and seemed slowly to accept that their mission to convert the world was over, that they no longer needed everybody to see things their way. In 1691 George Fox died. And after forty years of evangelism, violence and imprisonment, Quakers were never quite the same again.

Then and Now 1

Observing twenty-first century Quakers of my acquaintance and comparing them with their counterparts in the 1650s, I'm struck by numerous similarities, three big differences and one important question. Let's concentrate on the differences, because, while there are only a few of them, they are significant and they can cause confusion.

Modern Quakers reject the hectoring style of George Fox. They love much of what he said, but are embarrassed and frequently upset by the ways in which he said it. Alongside that difference, and perhaps more importantly, British Quakers in the twenty-first century are relaxed with the idea of uncertainty in their religious faith. They welcome doubt. They are not looking for answers.

That contrasts with Quakers of the seventeenth century, for whom certainty was a crucial element in religious life. But then again it was an essential for people of every faith and remains that way for many religious groups today, so I think it's important that it doesn't obscure what was so revolutionary and startling in the Quaker message. For all their lack of wavering, the Friends of Truth emphasised the centrality of personal experience, rejected creeds, would have nothing to do with religious ceremonies and turned their backs on the idea of sin. All this seemed scary and uncertain to the Christian believers who first heard it.

And that brings me swiftly to another important difference, which won't have escaped you if you've read the early sections of this book. The first Quakers, in common with virtually everyone else in the country at the time, were Christian. For many of their counterparts today, the Inward Light of Christ burns as brightly as it did for George Fox; others are interested in a rainbow of faiths. All regard their religion as something that is moving forward, never static. This tendency is a direct result of Quakers' openness to new ideas; and, while I'm sure that George would have difficulty in recognising the twenty-first century Friends he inspired, I'm equally convinced that he would have no trouble understanding the reasons for the change. Moreover, while modern Quakers are anxious to emphasise the Christian belief at the root of their faith, it's worth remembering that the kind of Christianity they are talking about was seen at the time as blasphemous and heretical enough to land around 40,000 of them in gaol.

The last major difference is the matter of dress and behaviour. George Fox disliked people to be 'flashy', as he frequently put it. Quakers dressed plainly and it wasn't long before their clothes resembled a uniform. Their black and grey, their theeing and thouing, made them visible in a way that Quakers never are today. Ordinary clothing and calling people 'you' has been the norm for a good century and a half now.

The similarities so outweigh the differences that it's unnecessary to list them: you already know what they are. Quakerism began in a spirit of protest and it has continued in that vein to the present day. As you'll see in a moment, its style changed during the three centuries that followed those first extraordinary forty years, but the impetus behind it did not. Openness to the spirit and being able to listen to the promptings of love and truth have been at the heart of Quakerism since it began.

And so to the important question. Would Quakers today have the strength, nerve and endurance to put up with the kind of persecution undergone by their predecessors? I can only say that I hope so. I think so. And in the next few pages, I'll attempt to lay down some markers to show how, during the quiet three hundred years that followed their inception, Quakers continued to tread a radical path.

Quakers and Conscience

George Fox's death might have been expected to leave a hole in the organisation of Quakers in Britain, but in the event their only loss was an emotional one: Friends were already well structured and used to teamwork. And the new century brought changes. British Quakers became quieter. They didn't feel the need to proselytise or preach or tell people they were right, so they began to acquire an anti-evangelistic attitude which has remained with them ever since. And they gradually found that, keeping their heads down, they were accepted as valued members of the wider community. In particular, they gathered a reputation in business for honesty and integrity. People started to notice, for example, that a child who was sent to buy a loaf from a Quaker bakery always came back with the right change. And, by the same token, the scales belonging to the Quaker butcher always delivered the right weight. Newly converted Quaker tradespeople frequently worried that they might lose money by being straight with their customers, but they were delighted to discover that the reverse was the case. Once seen as dangerous mavericks, Quakers became respectable. Some of them even got rich.

They handled their wealth with care. George Fox said, 'that which Friends speak, they must live in': Quakers put his dictum squarely into practice. They understood that religious truth (it gradually began to lose its capital 'T') extended to every aspect of existence. So they redirected some of the energy they had once used in caring for each other's suffering into working for the good of society as a whole. 'True godliness,' wrote William Penn, 'don't turn men out of the world but enables them to live better in it and excites their endeavours to mend it.' Quakers worked to bring about peace and social justice, because it was part of their religious impulse to do so. It was living in truth. There was no difference between the sacred and the secular.

Here is an example of an eighteenth century 'endeavour to mend', undertaken by a Quaker named William Tuke. It took place in York, where William was a tea importer. He became concerned when, in 1791, Hannah Mills, also a member of York Meeting, was admitted to the local asylum suffering from what they called 'melancholy'; it seems likely that we would describe it as clinical depression today. Members of the Quaker community tried to visit her, but were not allowed past the gates. Soon afterwards, they heard that Hannah had died in mysterious circumstances. Shocked at the veil of secrecy that hung over her final days, William had an idea: Quakers could open an institution under their own control, for the care and proper treatment of those who 'laboured under that most afflictive dispensation – the loss of reason'. It was, to put it mildly, an extravagant notion. He didn't really know what he was doing. He took the proposition to members of his meeting, but they were less than keen: some failed to see the point; others were of the view that it wasn't the business of Quakers to be founding psychiatric hospitals; most were clear that they simply knew too little about the subject to express an opinion.

William didn't give up. The plight of the mentally ill began to obsess him. He visited another institution, where he encountered a female patient who was forced to lie naked on a bed of straw, chained to a wall. The image haunted him. He couldn't let the matter drop. His passion became so intense that he went back to his meeting and asked them to reconsider. This time, having had an interval to ponder the urgency of his concern, the Quakers of York decided to go ahead and take a step into the unknown. Here is a part of their minute of 1792. I'm quoting it in detail because it glows with the optimism and progressive thinking of a small group of people who seem suddenly, in the stillness of their second business meeting, to have become visionaries.

> *That ... proper encouragement be given, ground be purchased, and a building be erected sufficient to accommodate thirty patients, in an airy situation, and at as short a distance from York as may be, so as to have the privilege of retirement; and that there be a few acres for keeping cows, and for garden ... which will afford scope for the patients to take exercise when that may be prudent and suitable.*

They decided to call their new project the Retreat, a name 'intended to convey the idea of what such an institution should be, namely a place in which the unhappy might obtain a refuge'. It finally opened in 1796. William tried to track down a suitably qualified person to be its first director (then called superintendent), but was initially unable to find anyone he could trust with the job. So, in the first year of the Retreat's operation, he did it himself. He discovered that his instincts had been right, that patients could be treated without being chained or locked up in squalor and that, crucially, mental illness was something from which a person could recover. When his new hospital had been open for twelve months, the right superintendent was found in a man named George Jepson. William continued to work as general manager (he called himself the treasurer) alongside George for twenty-three years until poor eyesight forced him into retirement at the age of eighty-eight. He died two years later.

The Retreat is still in York, still a Quaker institution and still a mental health provider, though it now concentrates exclusively on outpatient care. I've used it as an example because it demonstrates so much about how Quakers did things two hundred years ago and because, actually, nothing has changed: it remains the way they operate today. A person gets a powerful feeling that something is not right, not equitable, not – in a religious sense – truthful. That feeling may, as in the case of William Tuke, go against the grain of what mainstream society considers the right way to proceed. Indeed, when the person takes it to a meeting of their fellow Quakers it may not be entirely understood. But, as month follows month, the collective conscience is stirred. Light begins to dawn. And the minute written by Quakers at their moment of decision frequently conveys both anger at an injustice and the ability to move forward with determination to tackle it.

Only a few years after William Tuke was developing new methods of health care in York, a woman in London, Elizabeth Fry, was becoming deeply concerned about the prison conditions endured by women and children at Newgate Gaol. A Quaker banker's daughter, she had begun to take her Quakerism seriously in her late teens, but she was thirty-three and a mother (she went on to have eleven children) when she first began what was to become her life's work. On a visit to Newgate in 1813, she was horrified by what she saw: three hundred women in one room, sleeping on the floor without nightclothes or bedding, having to cook, wash and sleep in the same cell. She returned the next day with food and clothing for the prisoners, who were waiting to be transported to Australia. It was another four years before she was able to put her long-term plan into action, but when she started, she went at it headlong. She founded a little school for the children of the woman prisoners and provided knitting and quilting materials, so that they would have goods to sell when they arrived in their new country.

In 1818, she lobbied MPs, who eventually succumbed in 1823 by passing the Gaol Act. That improved conditions somewhat, though a good many of her comments ('capital punishment is evil and produces evil results') were roundly ignored. Elizabeth continued to work and agitate for improvements to the conditions of the women who were transported to Australia, ensuring that they were no longer chained during the voyage. She went on to found shelters for the homeless in both London and Brighton, as well as opening a nurses' training school. Much of what she strove for ('punishment is not for revenge, but to lessen crime and reform the criminal') is as relevant today as it was two hundred years ago.

Less proactive than William and Elizabeth in terms of the nitty-gritty of change and reform, but in some ways more significant in the development of Quakerism, was John Woolman. He was a mid-eighteenth century American from New Jersey whose view that 'conduct is more convincing than language' was a keynote for his life. He put spiritual principle first. In an age in which people undertook long journeys by coach and on horseback, for example, he preferred to travel on foot out of compassion for the animals. At a time when it was common practice to denigrate all religious faiths other than one's own, he chose to find 'no narrowness regarding sects'. At a point in history in which no one, including some Quakers, could see anything to criticise about the slave trade, John Woolman refused to have any truck with it, only ever wearing undyed clothing, for example, because coloured fabrics and leathers involved slavery in their manufacture and damaged the environment. He was a one-off.

It has been a great feature of Quakers that they have often

spotted something as an abomination long before the rest of the world. Such a case was that of John Woolman and the slave trade. It seems extraordinary that nobody could see just what an obscenity it was, but if we remember that it merely takes its place on a long list that today includes government-sponsored arms exports to battle zones, opposition to same-sex marriage and the compulsory use of tax for war purposes, it seems easier to understand that few people considered it to be as morally deranged as it was. Certainly, John Woolman was one of the first to understand its full implications and set about persuading other Quakers not to keep slaves. His style, however, was the exact opposite of the rabble-rousers of a century earlier. John's technique was to work at a personal level and to wait.

He tells a story in his journal of a time when a fellow Quaker asked him to prepare a will – he was a professional conveyancer – which included the wish that one of his sons should own his slave after his death. John Woolman agreed to do the job, but wrote the legal paper without including that particular bequest, explaining that he was unable to complete any document that contained such a clause. The journal continues:

> *I let him know that I charged nothing for what I had done, and desired to be excused from doing the other part in the way he proposed. We then had a serious conference on the subject; at length, he agreeing to set her free, I finished his will.*

His life was full of thoughtful interventions and his ability to sit quietly until a person was able to have a change of heart (recalling William Penn's 'wearing it as long as I could') has been an inspiration to Quakers ever since.

The ways of Quakers in John Woolman's America were virtually indistinguishable from those of their British counterparts; William Penn had imported his young faith more or less whole. As the nineteenth century dawned, however, things changed. There were splits and upheavals in the USA which altered how Quakers lived and worshipped there. The initial schism was between two groups, the first of whom, broadly evangelical, wanted more emphasis on the power and authority of Christian scripture, whereas the second emphasised their reliance on 'the promptings of love and truth in their hearts', to the exclusion of all else. Both of these were new paths for Quakerism and the resulting division, known as the Great Separation, caused disruption which continued for around seventy years on both sides of the Atlantic. In Britain, things had returned broadly to their original position by the end of the century, but in the USA it wasn't so simple. American Quakers identify themselves today as belonging to one of four traditions – 'programmed', 'evangelical', 'conservative' and 'unprogrammed' – and their manner of worship differs, too. There are meetings held in the way I have described in Part One; others, known as 'programmed meetings', are conducted by a pastor, with times for communal prayer, hymns and Bible readings, as well as silent worship.

In the eighteenth and nineteenth centuries, British and American Quakers of all traditions united in a common cause to end slavery. It was the first time that Quakers everywhere began to campaign on the same social issue. Their opposition had begun in Britain as early as the days of George Fox, though some, as we've seen, were not in unity with the rest. Things came to a head when, in 1761 in Britain and then in 1776 in America, meetings were held at which Quakers banned their members from owning slaves. They became the first corporate body in either country to condemn it. Because the British connection was essential to the existence of the slave trade, American Quakers urged their counterparts in the English capital to lobby parliament. It became a long, tortuous process. In 1783, British Quakers presented a petition to the House of Commons and followed it up with books, leaflets and letters to newspapers. Realising that society had little interest in them, they began to foster working relationships with several Anglicans, notably Thomas Clarkson (described by Coleridge as a 'moral steam engine'), which eventually resulted in the formation of the Society for the Abolition of the Slave Trade. And because Quakers were not allowed at that time to become members of parliament, they approached the evangelical MP William Wilberforce for support. There followed long periods of frustrating reversals, but finally in 1807, the British parliament abolished the trade in slaves and sixteen years later it became prohibited to own another person. Americans waited until 1865 for slavery to be banned in their country.

These campaigns are significant in the story of Quakerism for a number of reasons: firstly, for their uniting of every member in a common public cause; secondly for the clarity with which they demonstrate how essential it is to mix religion and politics (more about that in Part Three); and thirdly, fourthly and beyond, for the many ways in which they show how Quakers work for social justice. For example, they operate without leaders or agitators. Everyone who wants to be is involved. They demonstrate, lobby, leaflet and proselytise. They work with others to achieve their goal and have no interest in taking credit for what is eventually accomplished. They are not proprietorial, always content to leave a project in order to address something else of importance if they can see that things are thriving in the hands of others. Examples include Oxfam, Greenpeace and Amnesty International, all originally projects in which Quakers had a guiding hand and which now prosper without their explicit participation.

By the middle of the nineteenth century, Quakers began a gradual process of becoming less eccentric in their appearance. They wore normal clothes and many abandoned the 'thees' and 'thous' of earlier times. Both habits had become a kind of security blanket: less an overt symbol of their commitment than a way of keeping out the rest of the world. Their experience as anti-slavery campaigners showed how essential it was to avoid being treated as well-meaning oddballs. So, on both sides of the Atlantic it became usual, though by no means compulsory, for Quakers to look and behave in the same way as their neighbours. However, they were still excluded from much of society through no fault of their own. All non-conformists – that included Quakers – were forbidden by law to study at Oxford and Cambridge. Quakers' commitment to peace, part of their religious witness since 1660, ensured that they would not be joining the armed services. Nor were they permitted to become lawyers or, until 1828, to stand as MPs. So it was logical that the brightest, most enterprising Quakers would go into business. It was actually the only real prospect left and they proved to be brilliant at it.

The list of Quaker companies that became household names is long and impressive. There were bankers (Lloyd, Barclay), biscuit manufacturers (Huntley and Palmer, Carr), chocolatiers (Fry, Cadbury, Rowntree) and around 4,000 others, including Coalbrookdale cast iron and Clark's shoes. (Ironically, Quaker Oats has never had a Quaker connection:

the Ohio firm chose the name because they felt it embodied integrity, honesty and purity – a flattering decision, but not one that Quakers tend to boast about.) The founders of the Quaker firms – their religious heritage was well-known and often partly responsible for their success – became known for the quality of the service they offered and their skill in getting ahead. Some of their reputation was founded in the principled service, fixed prices and value for money that had so impressed customers in Quaker shops a century before. Still more was as a result of the enlightened ways in which they treated their staff: as soon as the Cadburys could afford it, for example, they built a model village for their workers, with a lido, free dentistry and cricket on the green. And much was simply rooted in the intelligence and business acumen of these entrepreneurs who, in another world, might have been lawyers, doctors, professors and ambassadors.

If Quakers in the late nineteenth century tended to inspire general respect, they got a more mixed reception from the public when Britain went to war in 1914. Many refused to fight. Others, around a third of the Quaker community in Britain, chose to enlist on the principle that it was the option that might bring peace more quickly. Either way, Quakers had a profound moral problem and inevitably acquired a reputation for cowardice. My own local meeting in London's leafy suburbs has contemporary records of up to eighteen doorkeepers being available for duty each Sunday in case of trouble from supporters of the war. Some conscientious objectors were shot, others were forced into uniform in the Non-Combatant Corps. The creation of the Friends' Ambulance Unit during the first year of the war gave an opportunity to 1,200 people, not all Quakers, to work as nurses tending the casualties of both sides, to ease the suffering of wounded soldiers on hospital ships and to establish their own scratch hospital at Dunkirk. It was an initiative that was revived twenty years after the end of World War One, when Britain declared war on Germany again in 1939.

World War Two divided both British and American Quakers once more, some of whom decided to fight. Most were objectors. The Friends' Ambulance Unit and the Friends' War Victims Relief Committee nursed wounded and sick people throughout Europe, as well as in parts of Africa, China, India, Burma and elsewhere. Their efforts were noticed. In 1947, The Nobel Prize for Peace was awarded jointly to Friends Service Council in Britain and Ireland and the American Friends Service Committee in the USA, in recognition of their relief work for victims of war. Quakers' reputation grew. I remember being told as a six year old in 1955 that 'Quakers are very good people'.

Then and Now 2

Being thought to be 'good' can be quite a headache. It puts people off. It gives them the idea they can never achieve the saintly heights of these paragons, so they'd rather not try. I know – and so will you when you come to meet some – that Quakers are exactly the same as any other group. There are the visionary ones, the hard-working ones, the delightful ones, the silly ones and the ones you don't agree with. That they can work together as well as they do appears sometimes to be in the natural order of things. At others it feels like a miracle.

The demographic of Quakers has changed considerably since 1947. I don't know of any academic study that might prove the point, but simple observation tells me that there are now fewer business people and a larger proportion of teachers in their ranks; not so many rich industrialists, more charity professionals on meagre pay. It means that money is tight. Where once Quakers could rely on hefty legacies to support their work, they now raise funds from their own membership and from Quaker grant-awarding bodies, often set up through the work of Quaker philanthropists who lived many years ago – the Joseph Rowntree Charitable Trust is an example.

They continue to use their resources with care and to be energised by the same spirit that emboldened their predecessors. In some respects, their interpretation of that spirit has made them less prescriptive than their forebears: British Quakers no longer prohibit smoking or drinking alcohol, for example (Advice 40 of *Advices and queries*), suggesting moderation in everything and leaving the definition of that to the individual. Their attitude to the arts, too, is entirely different from that of early Quakers. Painting, sculpture, dance, music and drama, while not having a programmed role in meetings, none the less have a significant part to play in the lives of modern Quakers, a fair number of whom are professional practitioners. Once seen as an artificial stimulant, a meaningless and luxuriant barrier between us and God, artistic endeavour is now seen as the polar opposite of that – a means of seeking and finding truth. And, while some of the nuances may have changed, that search remains at the heart of Quakerism. It is the lynch pin, 'the spirit of Christ by which we are guided'.

Many Quakers find themselves impelled as a result to become active in the fields of peacemaking, mediation, prison reform and social change. They work both with governments and at the grassroots, where things grow. But that kind of commitment is by no means the only way to be a Quaker. It is a faith that has many faces and I'll return to the theme in Part Three. There, I hope to look at what Quakers mean by sacramental living and how they find it impossible to distinguish between the sacred and the secular. Those twin themes lie at the heart of Quakerism and reach right back to the words of George Fox: 'Take off all oppression and set up justice over all.'

Part Three

Do we seek to be the channels of God's love and caring? Caring matters most.

EDWARD H. MILLIGAN, 1951

Deeds not Words

There's a big question often asked by people enquiring about Quakers. It comes in subtly different forms and in my experience it's frequently accompanied by a twinge of nervousness and expectancy. *Do Quakers believe in life after death? Do they believe we'll be reunited with our loved ones? What is their view of heaven and hell? How about the resurrection?*

These are vivid, urgent dilemmas for many of us. I've been asked about them so often and so earnestly that it would be wrong to write a book about the Quakers without addressing them directly. Yet, if you've read up to this point, you already know the only answer anyone can give: it depends on the individual. Quakers don't hand down creeds, so they are happy to discover their own views and beliefs about such matters. And, since Quakerism is an experiential faith, most of them are content to wait patiently until they are able to find out for themselves.

Some of the questioners are disappointed, because it isn't the response they were expecting. Maybe they already hold a belief in life after death. Perhaps they want to hear it confirmed as a corporate Quaker view. I'm sometimes surprised by that impulse, as if knowing that a lot of people are united in an idea would somehow confirm it as the one to have. But actually, this matter of eternal life is one about which Quakers as a body have nothing to say. While many of them faithfully believe – and some know with certainty – that there is something after death, others prefer not to let it worry them. The important thing is not to permit 'groupthink' to dictate matters of private faith or deny personal experience. Quakers do not believe what they are told.

There are other issues about which people have anxious questions. Some are about Jesus. *Did he ascend into heaven? Did he perform miracles? Did he die to save us from our sins?* Others explore the most pressing religious uncertainties of all. *How can God allow people to suffer? Where was the divine in the tsunami? Where was God in the pandemic?* In these dilemmas, it's important to be clear that, while it might be possible to hazard an educated guess at a majority response from Quakers in Britain, it wouldn't be helpful. It was William Penn who wrote, 'Speculative truths are ... to be sparingly and tenderly declared, and never to be made the measure and condition of Christian communion.' Quakers still agree with that: they avoid speculation, conjecture and guesswork in their religious lives. Many of them read extensively – modern biblical scholarship is a feature of the lives of a great number of Quakers – but they use experience and worship as their most reliable guides. George Fox put it succinctly: 'Every man, every woman then must come to the spirit of God in their own selves'.

Quakers are sometimes criticised for not having a clear theology. It is, by and large, a justified complaint. How could it be otherwise? They are also accused of being a pick-and-mix denomination, of allowing each person to create their own belief system by window-shopping their way around the world's religions, choosing an idea here and a doctrine there. That seems to me to be mistaken. Quakers have evolved a religious discipline over three and a half centuries, basing their corporate witness on the Inner Light within each individual. And they have evolved a number of shared testimonies – witness statements, in other words – which help them as they put their faith into action. That – the doing as opposed to the saying – is what Part Three is about. And to set it in context, I'm going to return briefly to Quaker worship and one or two more frequently asked questions.

Stained Glass Windows and Inner Light

Here are some more comments I've heard from first time visitors to Quaker meetings: *Silence is helpful, but I miss the hymns and church music. Why don't you have decoration or stained glass? And why no communal prayer? What's wrong with preparing what you're going to say? Wouldn't it be good to listen to a sermon once in a while?*

Having acknowledged a few lines ago that Quakers don't have much in the way of theology, I'm going to try to address those questions by invoking just a little now. Because, while Quakers have no corporate statement of belief, they are none the less united, all of them, in one great truth: that the human spirit gains resilience, courage and power as a result of direct communion with the spirit of the divine. It is the experience of Quakers that strength and grace come from guidance which is given when they live in single-minded contact with the force for good that many call God.

'Strength' is not a word commonly used in books on religion. Most faiths tend to concentrate on human weakness. Some of them believe that we are all innately guilty and emphasise our need to counter our ungodliness by living blameless lives. Everything possible must be done to avoid eternal punishment. For hundreds of years, churches have done all they can to provide resources to help people struggle against what they see as this natural fragility. They have constructed stunning buildings with glowing windows and gorgeous, vaulted ceilings to create an atmosphere of hushed devotion; commissioned music of soaring brilliance to inspire and comfort their congregations; provided teachers of wisdom and enlightenment to minister to them; created rituals that enable people to worship God in an atmosphere of safety and reverence. All this has been offered in a spirit of open-heartedness in order to support human beings in their frailty. It is a loving gift and I'm not disparaging it, but it is not the Quaker way.

Quakers do not deny human weakness, but their tendency is instead to give thanks for human strength. They believe in the essential goodness of people, so they deny the notion that we are by nature 'miserable sinners' and reject the habits and customs that go with it. While they appreciate the contribution to civilisation of religious art and culture, they know from experience that those kinds of aid may prove to be a barrier for them if they are used as part of their worship. They do not want religious ritual, symbol or costume to get in the way of their unmediated communion with the divine. It is in that relationship that they find their energy and spirit. They are not so much staring into the darkness, as standing in the Light.

Quakers do not proclaim what Christian churches call the Trinity – God the Father, God the Son and God the Holy Spirit

– but they talk often, and perhaps a little too vaguely, of 'living in the Spirit' and of being 'led by the Spirit'. So let's explore a little of what they may mean. The theologian H.A. Williams, not a Quaker, put it like this:

> *The Spirit is ourselves in the depths of who we are. It is me at the profoundest level of my being, the level at which I can no longer distinguish between what is myself and what is greater than me ... The Spirit is called God in me.*

Responding to the Spirit means opening myself up to possibility, allowing myself to be led, not deciding for myself. To do that, I have to trust that things will be well. That kind of faith only comes from experience: it can be scary not to plan my life. But slowly I learn to notice them, the thoughts that land in my head unbidden, the sudden impulses to do something unexpected. It may be a request from another person or a scheme of my own, but its clearest characteristic is that when it enters my mind I don't want it there at all. It's the opposite of what I fancy to be my next move. Then gradually, over days or weeks, I realise that what I fancy has nothing to do with it. I'll go along with the idea because of the way it came to me. I'll pursue it because it's there. And so I say yes to a fresh course of action because it seems to have come from inside my head and outside it at the same time. Then it works. It becomes part of me and I learn to love it.

Is this what is often called 'vocation'? Perhaps. Though in the context of this openness to the Spirit I might choose to pluralise the word. I've come to think of my day-to-day existence as a constant clustering of tiny vocations. And as they continue to multiply like cells under a microscope, they form a life in which my initial bouts of reluctance get swept away in the sheer delight of knowing that so much suddenly fits.

Here is Gordon Matthews, a present-day Quaker, quoted in *Quaker faith and practice* (and himself quoting Thomas R. Kelly in the first sentence):

> *How can we walk with a smile into the dark? We must learn to put our trust in God and the leadings of the Spirit. How many of us are truly led by the Spirit throughout our daily lives? I have turned to God when I have had a difficult decision to make or when I have sought strength to endure the pain in dark times. But I am only slowly learning to dwell in the place where leadings come from. That is a place of love and joy and peace, even in the midst of pain. The more I dwell in that place, the easier it is to smile, because I am no longer afraid.*

You may remember from Part One that *Advices and queries* suggests that we should listen to 'the promptings of love and truth' in our hearts and 'trust them as the leadings of God'. Finding the love and truth, not only in our own hearts but in those of everyone we meet, is at the heart of Quakerism. The Inner Light within each of us, 'that of God in everyone' as George Fox put it, is not something to be worshipped, but rather the spirit that allows people to accomplish things they would never have thought possible. That spirit is found not only in the stillness of worship, but also in a way of life often called – and not just by Quakers – 'living in the Presence'. It can be actively sought, this sense of direction. It can also arrive involuntarily. But by whatever means it comes, it is unmistakeable and gives us the strength to do what we least expected.

Faith in Action 1

You may have begun to get the feeling that everything in the lives of Quakers is inseparable from its spiritual roots. If so, you're right. This is a faith in which the religious and the everyday are identical, indivisible and without distinction.

People who try to answer that of God in everyone find that their lives alter as a result. When I first began to go to meetings, I remember telling a friend that 'these Quakers have got a lot to teach me about being in the world.' For a while, I worried that I was never going to be able to reach what I saw as 'their high standards', but I quickly learned that, far from trying to give other people a lot to learn or live up to, what Quakers actually do is pretty simple. They go to their meetings, listen to the message of Quakerism and spend the rest of their time putting it into practice as well as they can. At home, in the street, in the workplace, they are seeking to answer the Inner Light in others. They are looking on their fellow human beings as unique and precious. That does have to mean everybody, of course: not only family members and work colleagues, but also the ones in their lives they may not instantly warm to – the authority figures, the arguers, the critics, the naggers and brutes. They don't achieve anything like perfection – no one can and Quakers mess up just as much as anybody else – so it's by no means easy. But it is simple. And it changes everything.

In my own case, I noticed that I was involuntarily, often despite myself, beginning to listen to the points of view of others. That, I'm sad to say, came as a shock. I have a tendency to be dismissive of people I don't agree with: I can be intolerant and judgemental. It's not a helpful trait, to me or anyone else. Yet here I was, warming to opinions that were different from my own. I found myself weighing them, considering them, not discounting them so readily. It made my life easier. Another change, related to it, was that I could look at my own shortcomings with considerably less shame and more of a smile. 'There I go,' I'd think, 'being narrow-minded again.' And so my attitudes to my own behaviour were changing at the same time that I was acquiring more welcoming ways with other people. I wasn't being so hard on myself. Life started to become more of a pleasure.

An inevitable consequence of being more open-hearted was that I began to see that I was sometimes in a position to help other people. That may come as a surprise if you recognise yourself as someone who has always given generously. But again, I wasn't. So I sometimes startled myself with, say, an urge to talk to a homeless person shivering in a doorway, or a sudden inclination to help with a community project, or an itch to give money that I wasn't being asked for. It was basic stuff, nothing to get worked up about, but it was a change. Quakers are known to call the fruits of this impulse 'faith in action'. It's a grandiose term for the feelings I was experiencing, but I've used it as the heading for this section because I hope it will at least serve to show that what Quakers do to 'mend the world' is frequently not ground-breaking or heroic. Nor is it necessarily a response to an appeal. And it certainly isn't compulsory. It bubbles up unbidden from the inner core of people. They follow their noses. They do what they want to do. Seen in this light, living in the Spirit can be seen as no more than a logical consequence of taking other people seriously.

I have asked three friends to share a little of their experience:

I began worshipping with Quakers nearly three years ago. Week by week I've sat with Friends in silence, and this has gradually changed me. At times in the stillness I have felt the outward preoccupations of life dissolve into a state of simplicity where I glimpse a truth that is far greater than me. The preoccupations crowd around again, of course, but I retain a sense of truth at the centre and I am happy to talk about it to anyone who is interested – not to convert anyone but to open opportunities for others to explore their own experience of truth, or of the Spirit. I never spoke about my spiritual experience during thirty years as an Anglican. I had neither the clarity nor the strength that has come through the stillness.

I think religion occupies the ground where art, mental health and ethics overlap. Its particular contribution to ethics is extreme idealism—the idea that it could be worthwhile for a human being to give up their very lives, or at least their popularity, in support of something important. I haven't been called on to be a conscientious objector, but my Quaker grandparents were, and my Quaker father and aunt were, as also was my atheist mother. It is that background, coupled with hours in Meeting for Worship, that has me always thinking, 'Could I be doing better? Could we be doing better?' If there is one thing I feel clear about now it is the need for more manifest respect for everyone.

You might expect me to say that first I became a Quaker, then I learnt more about Quaker beliefs and principles, and then I tried to live them out. But it wasn't like that. I've always felt the need to try to care for others and give everyone respect – but not always been very good at it. It's more that I became a Quaker so that I could be part of a group that takes its beliefs and their practical implications seriously. My own attempts at treating people with equal respect at work didn't always seem to 'work' immediately, but having become a Quaker I felt supported in keeping at it. If I try to 'answer' what is good and true in another person, hopefully it will bring those qualities out. Even if it doesn't seem to work, this is how I should live. My faith is that it is worthwhile.

The last friend's idea that 'even if it doesn't seem to work, this is how I should live' is an eloquent description of the day-to-day existence of many Quakers. No one should expect perfection in themselves. In fact, I have never yet met a Quaker who has ever tried to be virtuous: they prefer simply to do what they can, knowing that feelings of shame and self-regard, of not ever being quite good enough, are out of place in a life lived in the Spirit.

Feelings of frustration and anger, on the other hand, are entirely appropriate when the ways of the world make it difficult to pursue such a life. For example, it's impossible to live truthfully if your employer expects you routinely to lie to customers as part of your job. Equally, you're going to have a hard time if you're asked to discriminate among people on grounds of age, or if you work for a company with money invested in the arms trade. You can't surrender moral responsibility for your actions because another person or agency has asked you to. They are yours. You must own them and be accountable for them. So Quakers have a long history of saying no to familiar behaviours that some of their neighbours might regard as everyday essentials.

A mindset of constant refusal, however, can make for a

negative attitude. So Quakers declare clearly to each other and to the world those things that they choose to say *yes* to: the fundamental principles at the core of all their lives and the actions and activities that result. These are the Quaker testimonies, and they are what the next few sections are about.

Testimonies

Let's return briefly to the Quakers of the 1650s. Testimonies began early in their history. There were behaviours and customs in society about which they needed to be assertive. An important one, as we saw in Part Two, was the bowing and curtseying and scraping and hat-doffing to one's social superiors, known as 'hat honour', that was a permanent feature of life in the mid-seventeenth century. It felt distasteful to the equality-minded Friends of Truth. Not only that, they considered it an offence against their religion because it came between them and their belief in 'the invisible power of God in everyone'. So they came up with a testimony, or corporate witness statement, in which they made it clear that, unless they were praying, they would keep their hats on their heads and not bow to anyone.

Another seventeenth century example before I move on to the present: a testimony evolved based on the fact that the days of the week and months of the year were named (they still are, of course) after Roman emperors and pagan gods. The early Quakers didn't like that, so they decided to call them 'First day', 'First month' and so on, because, as Christians, it mattered to them that they shouldn't be evoking heathen icons when they did something as simple as checking the date. These customs are rarely seen as being of spiritual importance to Quakers any more – though some do still adhere to them – and so the present-day Religious Society of Friends has chosen not to declare them as corporate testimonies that speak for Quakers in Britain.

So why have I begun to write about the testimonies with two examples that don't apply any more? For exactly that reason: they aren't in use by Quakers any longer because they've stopped mattering to them. So I hope I've made one thing clear at least: these principles shouldn't be mistaken for creeds.

Unlike statements of belief, testimonies slowly emerge as a result of the lives people are already leading. Quakers find themselves walking the same walk as each other, being inspired to take the same actions. With time, that particular walk, those particular actions, are seen to be evidence of a fundamental, everyday principle they all share. It becomes their testimony, their witness statement: a consequence of their convictions, not a starting point for them.

The early Quakers declared testimonies *against* certain ways of life. But the principles of activity and action that Quakers declare today are *in favour* of particular behaviours, attitudes and policies. They are: TRUTH, EQUALITY, SIMPLICITY, PEACE and SUSTAINABILITY.

These testimonies are 'umbrellas': they cover large numbers of everyday behaviours, as well as much weightier issues. Each is of vital importance to many individual Quakers, but not necessarily to them all. So, the testimony to peace, for example, speaks about the detail of our daily behaviour just as much as it touches the war-like ambitions of national governments. And the testimony to equality covers hundreds of initiatives: from same sex marriage to fair trade; from problems faced by people in prison to ethical investment.

It's an easy mistake – I know, because I've made it – to believe that something as central as, say, the Quaker peace testimony is a foundation stone of the faith. It may well be non-negotiable in the lives of some Quakers – it's turned out to be a determining factor in my own – but that doesn't mean that things have to be the same for everybody. Quakers don't impose their testimonies on anyone. Each is a pinch on the individual conscience, a religious imperative for each person, a response to what they consider, as woodworkers used to say, to be 'out of true'.

That word 'religious' is vital in all this. I often hear non-Quakers express surprise that the Religious Society of Friends is not a secular group (missing the clue in the name) because they associate it with peace and philanthropy and assume that's all there is to it. It really isn't. Quakers may be members of peace organisations, they may join colleagues in the fight for equal pay, work with their neighbours in initiatives to recycle waste – and they do – but their motives for declaring commitment to the Quaker testimonies lie deeper than matters of mere principle. They insist, for religious reasons, that their own lives bear witness to truth, equality, simplicity, peace and sustainability. The testimonies are not just beliefs, they are faith in action. They epitomise those words I quoted in the Prologue: *Attend to what love requires of you.*

A friend puts the situation well in what I regard as a perfect metaphor:

> *For me, the testimonies are not some kind of optional extras in my Quaker journey. They grow directly from my experience of a loving, healing, transforming power within and beyond me which I call God. Remember what it feels like when you have a hangnail or a bit of rough skin*

on your hand and you are asked to handle some delicate material like silk? The rough bit catches on the material – you can't not be aware of it. For me, testimony is the place in our lives where our experience of God's love and truth 'catches' on the everyday assumptions, frameworks and values of the world around us, demanding our attention and, often, our action. It is the place where God's kingdom breaks through into 'the world the way it is', opening the possibility – and the imperative – for change.

So when Quakers hear people say that religion and politics don't mix, they smile. For them, religion and politics, religion and peace, religion and truth, religion and equality, religion and simplicity, religion and sustainability are all mutually inclusive. The impulse of Quakers to 'mend the world' is a religious one. And if any one of these testimonies begins to speak to you in such a way that you start to take it seriously, to the extent that you see it as a deal breaker, that you even want to base your life around it, you are inevitably well on the way to thinking like a Quaker.

In the next few pages, I'll reflect a little on each of them. It is important to be clear at the outset that Quakers don't claim any kind of monopoly or exclusivity in these principles. They are shared by many other organisations and individuals, religious and not. What makes them work in the lives of Quakers is the blend of them, the acknowledgement of the ways in which they overlap, their affirmation that religion is indistinguishable from everyday life.

Truth

There's an old joke, a bit of a chestnut, that says a lot about Quakers:

> Q: How do Quakers sing hymns?
> A: Very slowly, because they're always reading the next line to see if they agree with it or not.

Gerald Priestland wrote in his excellent little book *Coming Home*, 'One thing you do not have to leave on the pegs in the Meeting House vestibule is your intellectual integrity'. It remains a great feature of Quaker practice that you never, under any circumstances, have to declare, affirm or intone anything that isn't true for you. Quakers rarely sing hymns, of course, but more to the point, they simply won't, either singly or in unison, tell any spiritual white lies that begin with 'I believe'.

As I'm sure you've already grasped, 'truth' means more to Quakers than not lying. It's a religious term, a way of expressing the principles behind how they behave and what they say yes to. Having said that, however, I can also confirm from my own experience that a decision to stop sidestepping the truth can be a good place to start a Quaker journey. My turnaround happened not long after my first meeting for worship. I'm sure there was a Quaker connection, but I don't remember anybody suggesting it. I think it was an idea that came to me in the stillness. I resolved to put an end to the fibbing I'd been making a habit of – no great whoppers, just a myriad little fictions and evasions, the kinds of thing, I persuaded myself, that everybody did from time to time. And I managed, more or less, to do it. I stopped. I spoke plainly and tried to do what I said I would. It was hard. It made me feel odd, not quite myself. Then I read a sentence by Thomas Merton from *No Man is an Island* that helped me to understand my difficulty. He wrote: 'We make ourselves real by telling the truth'. Yes, that was it. I understood it now. The unfamiliar queasiness was just me feeling real.

The simple stuff, like not embroidering facts and returning money when I had the wrong change, enabled me to take bigger, tougher decisions. I remember the first scary time that I found myself able to question a racist joke that I was told by a stranger: I thought I was going to get hit and felt anything but empowered. But then again, perhaps that in turn enabled me to turn down a lucrative job because its ethics sat awkwardly with me. I became significantly less fearful. And so I began to move into a mindset in which I worried less about reputation. I was able to set aside thoughts of failure, because success had a different meaning.

And even as I write this, I'm thinking, *Is that all truthful*? I think it is. *Have I put a gloss on it?* I don't think I have.

Like all Quakers, I'm an apprentice. It's vital to keep learning. I've discovered that, as with the other Quaker testimonies, truth works at its most potent level when it is combined with love. The plain speaking that is a refreshing feature of Quaker life only works when it's part of a desire to care for other people. *Attend to what love requires of you*. It isn't about one-to-one confrontations or, heaven knows, giving someone else a piece of your mind. It is having an instinct for what to say in a spirit of openness, sympathy and balance: a spirit in which the heart and the head are on the same axis. It is a testimony to truth, not to home truths.

If you want a simple exposition of its essence, you can do no better than to read Advice 17 of *Advices and queries*. I cherish it. Like all those little paragraphs, it blends uncomfortable reminders with a strong message of hope. I've personally found it helpful when, as can happen with me, I jump to conclusions or make detailed value judgements on the life of someone I don't know. Occasionally, it's a person who just happens to be walking by. *When words are strange or disturbing to you, try to sense where they come from and what has nourished the lives of others. Listen patiently and seek the truth which other people's opinions may contain for you.* When I'm told the very thing I don't want to hear, that last sentence gives advice that I need. And if I let my mouth run away with me and win an argument for the sake of it, I can try to remember not to *allow the strength of your convictions to betray you into making statements or allegations that are unfair or untrue.* Then there is the final clincher, eight words that for me epitomise this testimony to truth: *Think it possible that you may be mistaken.*

Some people describe it as being a testimony to truth *and integrity*. Advice 37 encourages Quakers to be honest in all they say and do. In other words, not just to tell the truth, but to *behave* the truth as well. If I'm behaving the truth, I won't speculate with money, either mine or other people's, in risky financial ventures. I won't invest my cash in ways that I know to be unethical. If I also embrace the Quaker testimony to peace, I won't be investing in any company that is involved with, or benefits from, the manufacture of arms – and depending on my ethical stance, that can whittle itself down to a surprisingly small number of organisations. And I won't kid myself that I'm making ethical investments when I'm not.

I won't be gambling my money away in the hope of sudden riches, either, since that represents a similar kind of speculation and is the antithesis of a fair day's pay for a fair day's work. It may not hurt me financially, depending on my bank balance and my ability to stop, but the dreams it engenders can damage me spiritually and emotionally; Quakers don't anchor their spiritual or emotional lives in things that are imagined. Being wrenched from the mindfulness of the present to a mirage in the future is like having a double standard of truth. It doesn't work for Quakers. As with their refusal to take oaths, what matters to them is to be the same on the inside as on the outside.

They expect just one standard of truth from governments, too, and agitate to get it. It was a Quaker, Milton Mayer in the mid 1950s, who coined the expression 'speaking truth to power'. Quakers have been talking plainly to rulers and their representatives since 1652 and continue to do so. The Quaker United Nations Offices in New York and Geneva work with governments and civil society for human rights, economic and climate justice and the peaceful resolution of conflicts. Quakers everywhere march and agitate, sometimes taking nonviolent direct action when they perceive that the need arises. Governments are just as capable as individuals, perhaps more so, of behaving in ways that are out of true. Quakers see it as essential to point it out as soon as it happens.

Early Quakers called themselves 'publishers of Truth'. The word had associations in the 1650s with what we might call 'reality' today. (It still survives in that form in some modern expressions – 'true north' and 'true grit' for instance.) But, as I pointed out in Part Two, they also used it almost synonymously with the word 'God'. That seems eccentric to us in the twenty-first century, so we're entitled to ask what was going on: was its use some kind of provocative play on words? Not exactly, but I do think that in speaking of truth and the divine in the same breath, the pioneer Quakers were making a point. They were saying that they had experienced

God as an authentic, creative presence in their lives; that their religion was grounded in reality, not in something fancied or imagined. So I find it helpful to look at the testimony to truth through the lens of that word 'real'. In the words of the Benedictine monk David Steindl-Rast: 'God is a name for a reality that cannot be named'.

If this is a testimony to what is real, it can help me choose some of my courses of action – do they represent reality for me? If not, I should acknowledge the fact and do something about it. The lifelong dream I have of winning a fortune on the horses – is there anything real about that? If not I can save my money. This claim of a government to be helping a nation by bombing it – is there a hint of reality in what they say? If there isn't, should I lobby and protest? Is my façade of politeness helping me to express what is real? If it's not, I might need to speak more plainly. These encounters I am having with a power outside myself – what, if anything, is real about them? If they are not imagined, perhaps I should do some serious thinking.

Equality

Quakers say (Advice 22) that 'each of us is unique, precious, a child of God'. Quakers' commitment to equality is an essential component of all their testimonies. You can't have truth, simplicity or peace without it. And, as with those testimonies, this one to equality is infused with love.

But what's the point, I've heard people say, when the world already knows that everybody is equal? We work hard as a society to turn our backs on racism, sexism and ageism. We have equal opportunities legislation. If Quakers are just agreeing with all that, why bother with a collective stance? You might just as well declare a testimony to brushing your teeth.

Quakers go further. *Attend to what love requires of you.*

Do all believers in equality extend it to people in prison? How many think that in almost every case separating offenders from society and suggesting they suffer some form of degradation is counter-productive? Are they happy for asylum seekers to live next door? Is everyone agreed that gay couples should be able to adopt and bring up children? Should prisoners have the vote? Should children and young people have an active say in the running of schools? Should prostitutes and sex workers be treated the same as the rest of us? Do we regard transgender people as suitable to undertake important state responsibilities? What do ninety-year-olds have to offer businesses, communities and organisations?

I vividly remember a 2005 television interview with an American second lieutenant in Iraq, who was intelligent, honest and direct in his responses. He was asked, 'Why do the invading forces call Iraqis "the Haji"? Why don't you use their right name?' He replied (I wrote down his answer as it was transmitted), 'You have to desensitise yourself from them. That's why we call them "Haji." If you start thinking about them as human, then my God, how are you going to kill them?'

I found it a ghastly, but also in its way surprisingly refreshing remark. His answer was truthful and clear. How, indeed, can you kill someone if you can imagine their mother, husband, or children? How can you shoot a person if you are able to look into their eyes? How can you murder another human being if you believe they have that of God within them, if you believe that we all possess the Inner Light? It is so much easier if you give them a name that removes their soul.

We like to treat people who threaten our equilibrium as 'other', because it's easier for us to objectify them. And we don't have to be trying to kill them to do it. As we know, there is always a name for people we regard as stupider, dirtier and less well-dressed than we are. Fifty years ago in Britain, it was 'gippos'; then it was 'chavs'. More recently 'trailer trash' has been imported from the USA. We need to ensure that other people are different and laughable. Over the years, the British have become inured to hearing about chinks and wogs, nerds and hooray henrys: as one name becomes unacceptable, another takes its place.

Quakers are not perfect – they have sometimes taken a while to implement much needed change – but they try to reject the stereotypes. Men and women work together and are given the same and equal responsibilities, with no jobs reserved either for them or their gender. They aren't called 'Mr', 'Mrs' or 'Ms' – first and second names work fine for Quakers. And children are considered to be valued members of the community in the same way as their parents, doing jobs within the meeting if they wish to. Trans and non-binary people are welcomed unquestioningly. Men and women serve their Quaker meetings until they choose to stop and if physical circumstances or old age make things difficult for a person, everything possible is done to help.

I remember being a member of a committee alongside a woman whose valued contribution was threatened when she had a fall and lost a little of her mobility during her eighty-eighth year. The biggest problem was that she found it difficult simply to get to the committee room, because it was up a flight of stairs. Another member offered the ground floor of his house for the meetings, which continued uninterrupted.

At the end of her three-year stint on the committee, when she was coming up for ninety, she decided that it was time to lay down her active Quaker work, but she continued to offer the committee's clerk the fruits of her experience by phone. Age is not a barrier to an active life.

None of this seems odd to Quakers, but it might be considered unusual in some churches and organisations. Christians who have a problem with women or gay people being priests and bishops are inevitably going to find the ways of Quakers distasteful, but then the concept of 'the priesthood of all believers' runs so deep in the Religious Society of Friends that debates are likely to founder long before they reach details of gender or orientation. It is in some of their 'endeavours to mend the world' – for example, in matters of criminal justice and prison reform – that Quakers are frequently seen to be beyond the pale. They are more interested in healing than retribution, more keen to achieve rehabilitation than punishment and far more concerned to achieve a balanced outcome than a tit-for-tat. If you want to know about the kinds of project that interest Quakers in this field, I suggest you begin by investigating some of the organisations in which they have had an input – perhaps beginning with Circles of Support and Accountability (www.circles-uk.org.uk), Quakers in Criminal Justice (www.qicj.org) and the Restorative Justice Council (www.restorativejustice.org.uk).

The plight of refugees and asylum seekers is a great concern of Quakers. They simply don't accept that any single person or group of persons is deserving of less respect than another. So when asylum seekers and failed immigrants are left for years in detention centres, it sparks a reaction in Quakers that won't be stilled. They work on their behalf, lobbying government, organising petitions, trying to persuade their fellow citizens that everybody is deserving of the same respect: The Quaker Asylum and Refugee Network (www.qarn.org.uk) will tell you more.

The spirit that fires these projects, as well as many more like them, is the same one that energised nineteenth century Quakers in their demands for the end of slavery. And just as their views were considered extreme, so are modern Quakers sometimes thought to be bizarre and unconventional in the inequalities they notice and the work for social justice that ensues. But for Quakers, it's a simple matter of caring for others. If you regard the rest of the world, everybody you meet, as truly equal and if you also see it as a religious matter, based on the light of God being found in every person, you share a Quaker view. If you also find the testimony to truth empowering, you are beginning to discover a duality which lies at the heart of the Quaker faith. Those two testimonies, truth and equality, are the quintessence of it all. From them grow the testimonies to simplicity and peace. Without truth and equality, simplicity is little more than an advertiser's gimmick. Without truth and equality, peace is just a politician's promise.

Simplicity

The designer William Morris wrote a sentence that meant so much to Quakers in the early twentieth century that they included it in their generation's edition of *Advices and queries*: 'Have nothing in your house that you do not know to be useful, or believe to be beautiful'. It no longer appears in current versions, but it still has resonance for Quakers, who tend not to be comfortable with gaudiness and tat, either in clothing, goods or choices of entertainment. Times change and the homespun styles that they sported in the late twentieth century are less in evidence among their younger counterparts in the twenty-first; but a distinct lack of interest in fussy self-indulgence continues.

While I'm dwelling briefly on the topic of design, it may be useful to be clear that Quakers are not Shakers, so none of that old world, functional look so beloved of the furniture industry is attributable to them. Nor are they Amish – a surprisingly common confusion – so suggestions that Quakers are out of touch with their century or reluctant to use electricity are misplaced. They are as connected with contemporary life as anyone else, welcoming of innovation and relaxed with modern technology. There's no rule that says Quakers have to leave the world alone or turn their back on any particular style. These are matters of personal taste and discernment. Quakers make their own choices in every aspect of their lives. And in doing so, they are led in their distinct and individual ways by the testimonies.

All the Quaker testimonies are at some level about the things that block us from God: this one to simplicity is about nothing else. *Attend to what love requires of you.* It suggests that it's a bad idea to become involved in anything that we know will get in the way of a clear and unmediated relationship with the divine. It doesn't make sense to allow a car or a necklace or an enjoyment of luxury (or, for that matter, an altar or a ritual or a piece of stained glass) to damage our ability to see the way forward in our religious lives. For some people, the car or the ritual may ease their path or at least provide no obstacle to it. For others, they form a barrier. So it's about taste and personal choice but, more importantly, it's about listening for the promptings of love and truth in our hearts.

Such promptings have a lot to tell us about the ways in which we decide to spend our money. Many Quakers, unwilling to fork out cash on possessions that they regard as trivial and unimportant, prefer instead to direct their earnings towards things they believe to matter more. So, if I'm an employer, it could make sense to think about ploughing some of my profits into providing better conditions in the workplace. If I'm an employee, it might be preferable not to pursue a lucrative promotion that takes up time I can use effectively elsewhere. If I'm an entrepreneur, I might consider using my gifts to work for a charity as well as what I normally do. If I can afford to save money for a pension, it might be sensible to consider early retirement in order to spend time on projects that help others and give me fulfilment.

Quakers challenge the materialism of society. At the same time, they are not afraid to look hard at the way they live themselves, questioning their own needs and trying not to exceed them. This doesn't mean that they refuse to eat well, take holidays or enjoy themselves. Quakers are not killjoys. But they think carefully about the balance of what they spend on themselves as opposed to others and they tend to avoid extravagance. They are alert, too, to the artificial creation of new desires by an advertising industry that feeds off people's reluctance to look reality in the face. Quakers are as fallible as anyone, of course. I know many – I am one – who would like to do better at living within their needs as opposed to their wants. But they do keep trying.

And they query the extent to which a comfortable lifestyle may be achieved at the expense of people who are not able to benefit from the prosperity enjoyed by rich minorities. They are careful not to endorse activities that may harm the environment or hurt other human beings. They often quote a sentence attributed to Gandhi: *Live simply in order that others may simply live.* And paragraph 41 of *Advices and queries* adds to it by saying that we, not just 'others', are likely to make gains from the change: *Try to live simply. A simple lifestyle freely chosen is a source of strength.* That, it seems to me, is where the heart of this testimony lies. It isn't just about whether to sell the car or cancel the fancy holiday. Those may be part of the journey, but they are not the point. This testimony helps us to avoid abandoning our identity. By living simply enough to understand who we are, we gain strength. We are able to concentrate on the things that matter.

In *The Man in the Sycamore Tree*, Thomas Merton, a Trappist monk, wrote:

> *If you want to identify me, ask me not where I live, or what I like to eat, or how I comb my hair, but ask me what I am living for, in detail, ask me what I think is keeping me from living fully for the thing I want to live for.*

Quakerism, unlike some religious faiths, doesn't tell us what to live for. Only we can find that. But in the stillness of its worship – an important aspect of this testimony – we have a holy space in which to explore. I spent a lot of time worrying about simplicity when I first started mixing with Quakers. I felt intimidated. I knew that I had alterations to make in my busy, complex, abstracted life but I didn't know where to begin. It was through Quaker worship that I began to understand that I didn't necessarily have to alter the externals first. In fact, it was better for me to work from the inside. I allowed myself to change and felt my priorities shift. I began to see the Quaker testimonies as an invitation to live adventurously. And in doing so, I started to understand what keeps me from ‘living fully for the thing I want to live for’. Now, years later, my life is simpler. It has been an unpredictable and fulfilling aspect of my spiritual journey.

Peace

There are a lot of ways of seeing the peace testimony: a lot of windows, if you like, into the same room. Conflict transformation; the arms industry; nonviolence; peacemaking; the relief of suffering in battle; the determination never to lift an impatient finger to a child; conscientious objection; pacifism; an end to state killing; an end to state torture: to name but ten. No one can be committed to activism in all those spheres, but we can know what we think and, who knows, we may find ourselves thinking so deeply that we start to care. Caring can lead us to make connections. If we already know that truth matters to us as a religious imperative, it follows that we can't fight a war, because warfare and truth are mutually exclusive. And if equality has become an all-encompassing necessity for us, we can't kill another person or allow them to be killed in our name. So, if only on the basis of those last two testimonies and some simple logic, there is a chance that peace will become something of profound importance. Some of us may turn into energetic campaigners. That's how it is with Quakers.

When I first got interested in Quakerism, this topic worried me more than any other. If you're already a member of the Peace Pledge Union or Peace Direct or connected with a peace movement in some other way, it's unlikely that you'll share the difficulties I had. But I was one of those who think that ‘war is a dirty job but someone has to do it’. As long as it was happening far away and I was able to keep my eyes tightly shut, I could pretend that I didn't bear any responsibility. 'And anyway,' I thought, 'sometimes you have to meet force with force.' I don't think I was alone. Newspaper editors understand the value of portraying all military action as heroic, and politicians know how many millions of votes there are in calling their adventure a 'just war'.

It was thinking about that flawed mental construct, the just war, that started my change of mind. As I sat in the silence of Quaker meetings, I began to see things differently. Was it that I thought you had to be a pacifist to be a Quaker? If so, I was wrong. Was it that I was sitting in a room week after week with people who were thinking deeply – more deeply than I ever had – about these matters? Probably. Whatever the reason, I began at last to separate in my mind the *cause* from the *war*. And it made all the difference. There are many just causes, I realised, but there is no just war. If you believe there is that of God in everyone, you have to find solutions that don't involve the justification of mass murder. There are other, better ways and it's our duty to channel public money towards helping skilled peacemakers to find them, rather than perpetuating the myth that only combat professionals know how to deal with violent conflict.

At the same time as I was having these changes of heart, a quotation from G.K. Chesterton, a Roman Catholic, hit me hard: 'The Christian ideal has not been tried and found wanting. It has been found difficult; and left untried.' As I read those simple sentences, I was overwhelmed by a feeling that here was a truth I had always known but somehow never dared to acknowledge. It reached the bottom of my soul. And, in my vivid reaction, I started to realise that I was living out religious impulses I had been experiencing for years, but at a subconscious level. I began to look again at the peace testimony, but this time as a purely spiritual matter. The practical issues of war and conscientious objection became less pressing. I could no longer tolerate the thought of other humans being destroyed in my name. In the words of William Penn: 'A good end cannot sanctify evil means; nor must we ever do evil, that good may come of it.'

In rejecting violence, I haven't necessarily turned my back on the use of force. I see force and violence as being different from one another. They have different effects. Whatever its intention, violence depraves and corrupts: it is counter-productive, because its aim is to destroy. The considered use of force, on the other hand, may not be destructive and can work for the common good. So I am able to accept that the forcible restraint of one person may sometimes be necessary to save the life of another. But I won't be drawn on hypothetical scenarios and imagined challenges (the ones that begin, 'Suppose you saw someone threatening your sister with a knife...?'), because they have no bearing on a reality I understand. The truth is that no one can be sure of what they might do in those circumstances. Instead, I have to concentrate on the realities I know. And at the top of my list is a precious reality that simply refuses to go away: the sanctity of human life. Once I believe in that, I must continue to believe. No exceptions. I can't lay the sixth commandment ('thou shalt not kill') to one side for set periods of time and then pick it up again when it suits me. I either think it is right or I don't. So, in my first year of attending Quaker meetings my position changed from tacit acceptance of the status quo to a conviction – as yet untested, of course, because I've never been asked to join an army – that, for religious reasons, I would be a conscientious objector in times of war.

The domestic issues of daily life, however, have proved a valuable testing ground. I grew up in my teens and twenties to be an explosively angry person at times of conflict, often handling the familiar tussles of everyday life without consideration or calm. After thirty odd years of messing up, I took the decision in middle age to do things differently. Through much trial and a lot of error, I slowly acquired the ability to forgive myself and move on from my old ways, and in the process I made some useful discoveries. I learned that conflict is inevitable and not something to withdraw from – it is, after all, what makes the world go round – and so I have no choice as to whether or not I confront it. Where I have complete freedom is in how I *handle* the conflict. And I made a personal breakthrough in realising that – irrespective of my religious impulses – an instinct to be violent and shouty when presented with a tough situation was less effective in solving problems than its polar opposite. Nonviolence is a better coping mechanism for me than violence. It works. It is a positive response to challenges. So, I gradually changed my behaviour. Quakers taught me that the most effective way of renouncing violence is to become actively nonviolent. I brought up my children without shouting or smacking, I rarely raise my voice in anger these days, and I usually manage to maintain respect for those who disagree with me. A lot of small decisions have led to a few big consequences.

I've drawn on a little of my own life because it shows the kinds of change that can sometimes happen to people who go to Quaker meetings. I understand that my experience may not be yours, and you don't, of course, have to share my opinions for Quakerism to make a difference to you. Nor do you have to be any kind of activist. If, as was the case with me, you don't quite know what your viewpoint on the peace testimony is, you might let the experience of being with Quakers help you find out. Talk to them. They love the subject, while by no means necessarily agreeing with each other all the time: some, for example, believe that limited military action may be essential in certain instances, while others find that idea to be anathema. Still more, unsurprisingly, stick to one of the hundreds of viewpoints in between.

But this talk of conscientious objection and personal change is far from most Quakers' everyday experience of the peace testimony. For them it is about personal attitudes, about peacemaking, mediation and conflict resolution. There is a statement, probably originally made by Gandhi but now attributed to a host of iconic leaders (I once saw it claimed for Picasso) that states the position perfectly: *There is no way to peace. Peace is the way.* And it was reworded in the title of Thich Nhat Hanh's fine book: *Peace is Every Step.* It was also the essence of that first poster I saw, quoting the Quaker Sydney Bailey: *Peace is a process to engage in, not a goal to be reached.* It is something to do every day. There is no end, no target, no victory. Peacemaking becomes a constant, rewarding way of life. And so Quakers have a history of setting up projects dedicated to the resolution of conflict. Here are two that tell some of the story:

The Alternatives to Violence Project (known as AVP) was started in 1975 by a group of inmates at Green Haven Prison in New York as an experimental workshop in collaboration with local Quakers. It spread throughout the prison system, and eventually into mainstream society. It now consists of a worldwide network of volunteer groups whose goal is to reduce the level of violence in society by providing workshops in which people can learn nonviolent methods of resolving conflict. In Britain, there is an extensive programme of work in schools, prisons and workplaces, as well as weekend workshops for individuals and communities. You can find more information at www.avpbritain.org.uk.

Leap Confronting Conflict is a British-based organisation established in 1987, specialising in conflict among young people. Their aim is to prevent the escalation of everyday conflict into violence. They deliver their work through community and school based projects, always in local partnerships. They are supported by more than fifty specialist trainers around the UK, many of whom are young people themselves. They have a holistic approach to conflict resolution and a distinctive training style, tackling everyday interpersonal conflict, group offending, knife crime, bullying and racist violence. Like AVP, they don't stress their Quaker beginnings. They can be found at www.leapconfrontingconflict.org.uk.

These two examples can only scratch the surface of the initiatives through which the testimony to peace is expressed. There are many others, some Quaker and some not, and still more that have Quaker roots no longer routinely acknowledged. Conscience, the peace tax campaign (www.conscienceonline.org.uk) is one example, lobbying for the legal right of conscientious objectors to have the entire military part of their taxes spent on peace building. The Campaign Against Arms Trade is another (www.caat.org.uk), working to end the international trade in arms. And Amnesty International (www.amnesty.org.uk), an initiative originally with Quaker connections, continues in its aim to 'protect people wherever justice, fairness, freedom and truth are denied'.

Quakers don't have a rule, of course, that says they must be active in all this – it's entirely up to the individual. However, there's one sentence in *Advices and queries* that can be said to apply to each of us, both Quaker and not. It's part of Advice 31 and quotes John Woolman, the American visionary we met in Part Two: 'Search out whatever in your own way of life may contain the seeds of war'. And it echoes some words of George Fox, who talked of living in 'the virtue of that life and power that takes away the occasion of all wars'.

It's possible, as we go about our business every day, to take decisions that work for change. What we buy, what we use, what we read, who we listen to, what we say: it all matters. This business of peace is for us to work out in our own lives, just as much as it is for others to fix in our name. *Attend to what love requires of you.*

Sustainability

If the peace testimony encourages us to live our lives in ways that do not contain the seeds of war, Quakers' concern for care of the earth is about a way of behaving that does not contain the seeds of destruction. The parallels are plain. Both uphold the rights of every community to enjoy an equal share of what the earth has to offer. Both bear witness to a tendency in us all to extinguish life through selfishness and avarice. Both acknowledge the necessity of balance and wholeness. Both are concerned with the building of community and understanding through common values.

When I began writing this book, I asked some friends to identify the issues that mattered most to them as Quakers. One responded immediately:

> *Mankind is rearranging the world and its resources to suit perceived needs and feed greed. Happily, Quakers*

are now evolving a testimony to the care of the earth and the environmental issues that are involved in that. But there is an interdependence among the testimonies. You cannot, in my view, pick out one and leave aside the others. People will say that the peace testimony can stand on its own – but how can they justify that, when the world's conflicts are driven by inequality, hunger and injustice? The unequal distribution of resources per head as between, say, Africa and the USA is scandalous, while we are now threatening to affect the food resource by growing crops to provide fuel for the western world.

In speaking of Quakers 'evolving' a testimony, he chose his words carefully; there was a lack of clarity for many years around whether Quakers should declare a testimony to sustainability. (There was disagreement, too, as to the appropriateness of the word 'sustainability' itself, since it has so many meanings and interpretations – I take as my guideline a definition by the UN's Brundtland Commission in 1987: 'Meeting the needs of the present without compromising the ability of future nations to meet their own needs'.) Nowadays it's true to say that every Quaker I meet is passionately convinced of the need to do more, much more, at both a personal and community level, to help avert global catastrophe.

Continuing to find new ways to live sustainably is a constant commitment for Quakers. And, as with the first four testimonies, they regard the issue as a religious matter. Quakers see all persons as holy, and they question accepted notions of equality. So, confronted with a crisis that exposes lack of care for the spiritual well-being of people, social and cultural divisions among communities, and negligence of the welfare of future generations, they respond by emphasising the need for action. *Attend to what love requires of you.* The task before them, before all of us, is to abandon status, unearth our innate generosity and unselfishness, and prioritise people who are as yet unborn. Quakers know that, adapting Gandhi's statement on peace a few pages ago, there is no way to sustainability: sustainability is the way.

The Quaker testimonies to truth, equality, simplicity and peace developed slowly, from passionately held concerns of small groups of individuals to corporate witness statements that spoke and still speak for Quakers everywhere. Their organic growth can be clearly observed with hindsight. John Woolman was perhaps the first Quaker to take a personal stand on caring for the environment. In his diary for 1772, he wrote, 'The produce of the earth is a gift from our gracious creator to the inhabitants, and to impoverish the earth now to support outward greatness appears to be an injury to the succeeding age'. I find it sad to contemplate that the ground-breaking Quaker entrepreneurs of the eighteenth and nineteenth centuries were in some cases responsible for the very damage he was talking about. Abraham Darby, for example, a British pioneer of metal manufacture and a notable herald of the industrial revolution, was already producing pig iron in coke-fired blast furnaces sixty years before Woolman made his forlorn, prophetic observation. As in so many aspects of his thinking, the American was years ahead of his fellow Quakers and centuries ahead of his time.

The great Quaker entrepreneurs can hardly be blamed for failing to grasp the long-term effects of their labours. They shared with Woolman a belief in the unity of all creation, a respect for the earth, an acceptance of the sanctity of life and an understanding that the human footprint on the globe should be a light and undamaging one. Their twentieth century counterparts held all those convictions, but were as slow as the rest of the world in catching on to the ruinous effects of industrialisation. Greenpeace, for example, was founded in 1971, but it was already 1988 by the time British Quakers made their first clear corporate statement acknowledging that the globe stood on the brink of a disaster:

> *Our planet is seriously ill and we can feel the pain. We have been reminded of the many ways in which the future health of the earth is under threat as a result of our selfishness, ignorance and greed. Our earth needs attention, respect, love, care and prayer.*

This pronouncement coincided with the United Nations Intergovernmental Panel on Climate Change and shows alertness to the depth of the problem. But while many individual Quakers responded to the news of impending catastrophe with a personal commitment to action, their collective response remained muffled. It was another twenty years before the British Quaker community began to unite on the issue.

In August 2011, Pam Lunn, a programme leader at Woodbrooke Quaker Study Centre, gave a talk to an assembly of around a thousand Quakers at their annual gathering, known as Yearly Meeting (described in Part One). She called her lecture *Costing Not Less Than Everything*, a quotation from T.S. Eliot that conveys the flavour of her uncompromising message. She spoke graphically of the depth of the crisis, of a worsening global economic environment, failures of infrastructure and interruptions in supplies of energy, food, goods and services. But this was not an hour of negativity and gloom. She made practical propositions. She suggested that when such temporary glitches occur, we should treat them as practice for a future in which they are certain to become everyday facts of life. She was positive in encouraging her audience to take personal responsibility in making whatever changes may be called for, but she also acknowledged the necessity for people to work together. Emphasising the need for spiritual impulses to be turned into action, she urged Quakers in Britain to become 'truly a low carbon community'. Here is a passage from the book (full details are in Appendix One) issued to accompany the lecture:

> *Quakers are needed ... to be faithful to Quaker testimonies; needed to be visible, to be speaking out, to be offering leadership; needed to do what is right in the face of external pressing circumstances. To use Gandhi's phrase, Quakers – individually and corporately – need and are needed to "be the change we wish to see in the world". To do and be so will require us to deepen our spiritual grounding, alone and together – not only for the sake of inward exploration but for the future of human society. A further challenge will be to find the corporate will, the rediscovery of a depth of corporate discipline, to undertake this wholly and fully, not just as a matter of piecemeal personal choices.*

ßThe gathering united behind the message and Quakers in Britain pledged themselves to action, to 'a strong corporate commitment to become a low carbon sustainable community'. The minute of the meeting continued, 'The process needs to be joyful and spirit-led', adding that Quakers 'keep it in their hearts that this action must flow from nowhere but love'.

In recent years Quakers have continued to develop their commitment to sustainability. They know from their history that it is the process that matters, the daily routine of putting one foot in front of the other: not looking for handy goals, so much as faithfully practising spiritual discernment. Only through an attitude of acceptance, with equality and simplicity as our watchwords, can any of us prepare for the massive shifts in openheartedness and generosity that are needed now, this minute. They will inevitably have to become a way of life for future generations, as the world crisis is tackled daily. So, we are back where we began. As we prepare for greater selflessness and the breaking down of cultural barriers, as we look for resources to enable the human spirit to flourish in the face of possible global disaster, we are reminded once more that the whole of life is sacramental.

Faith in Action 2

There's a story that Quakers sometimes tell to explain the connection between the silent meeting and the work they do in the world.

A newcomer walks into a meeting for worship late and is confronted by a room full of people, all sitting silently. He pauses in awkward anticipation. 'When does the service begin?' he asks. 'When the meeting ends,' comes the reply.

As improving tales go, it's a bit on the smug side, it seems to me – and I hope the Quakers you meet are kinder to you than that – but it does contain an essential truth. As the meeting comes to a close, the real work begins. As we've seen, Quakers are under no pressure to do anything and the impulse to give service may take a long time to bubble up, but it does frequently appear. How does it happen? It's channelled through the mindfulness and love that are the quintessence of Quaker worship. They are the same mindfulness and love that characterise Quakers' work in the world and they are carried forward from the meeting house into the everyday. It becomes a continuum. In time, it's impossible to distinguish one from the other.

A quest for meaning is at the core of every religious faith. For Quakers, meaning lies not only in the revelation of great truths, but in finding a purpose and fulfilling it, in taking action that may help someone else. So, meaning and purpose become the same thing. Meaning becomes purpose, purpose becomes meaning, and it's hard to say where one ends and the other begins. And they have nothing, absolutely nothing whatever, to do with sacrifice. This whole process is about delight. It's the joy of meeting other humans in the spirit, the exhilaration of being in the right place at the right time, the thrill of offering one's heart and soul.

It's not a phenomenon, of course, that is exclusive to Quakers. Many other religious and secular groups report exactly the same responses. Being in the world, working for others, joining the struggle for social justice, helping to resolve conflict: these are some of the ways in which people of all faiths and none find not only meaning, but also purpose. For Quakers, there are many such initiatives. Some undertake groundbreaking schemes: founding charities, helping the homeless, giving advice to refugees and asylum seekers. Others organise soup runs for people living on the streets, organise peace vigils, work in prisons, read to patients in hospitals. Still more give service to their own Quaker meeting, ensuring that it can function at a day-to-day level. And a large number put into practice, in their workplace, housing estate or street, principles of mediation and conflict resolution that they have learned through mixing with other peacemakers.

I've asked some friends to write a few words about the kinds of thing they find themselves inspired to do. I don't want to suggest that their experiences are necessarily typical or representative of the ways in which Quakers behave, but I hope you may find them intriguing. You'll notice a wide variation in their activities, from everyday experience to large projects, none any less or more important than another.

When I retired, people advised me not to fill every hour with activity: wait, they said, for the right things to come along. In our local paper, an advertisement said the Youth Offending Team wanted volunteers. This spoke directly to me: I felt a clear leading to apply and was accepted for the work. As a sociology and religious studies teacher, I had taught that faith communities advocate helping offenders to reform and to make reparation to society. As a Quaker, I was clear that offenders were unique, precious children of God and that our testimony to equality demanded that they be helped in a positive and humane way. My experience of working with young offenders has convinced me that people do have that of God in them, that this can be reached and nurtured and that they can change for the better.

At the heart of my work for peace lies the belief that there is something of God in all of us; we are all precious and unique, all able to contribute our particular gifts generously to the world. This means being non-judgemental, softening and opening to hear each voice, our own as well as others. Then maybe we can each see from different perspectives and get beneath the surface to our different fears and needs. And we can also learn more about ourselves and hear ourselves as others hear us. The first time I realised what this means was when I organised a meeting for six traffic action groups who disagreed fiercely about the solution to the huge increase of cars in our neighbourhood. I invited each of the twelve representatives to speak for five minutes about their fears and needs and after a few protests and interruptions, they discovered the value of it. Anger gave way to a palpable wave of relief, as each voice was seen to belong to a real person. But the question on my mind now is: How can I apply this open, soft practice in political campaigning?

Some years ago I became aware of women working in street-based sex work in London. The first woman I came across was sleeping in doorways on Dalston High Street. She was pregnant, HIV positive, had TB and ulcers. She wasn't registered with a GP and wasn't even getting pain killers. She described a life of violence, loneliness and fear where crack, when she could get it, gave her a brief respite from pain. She had a learning difficulty as well as having been traumatised. It seemed that if her mental health wasn't taken care of, nothing would change. Sadly she wasn't alone and I went on to set up Street Talk, a registered charity which takes mental health care to women in street sex work and to women who have escaped from trafficking. I like working with very poor people because I find them honest. They have a greater generosity than the rest. And I include myself among the rest.

Having worked most of my adult life on energy and climate policy I'm now with the Quaker charity Living Witness, supporting Friends and Meetings addressing sustainability. Central to our work is strengthening spiritual community through listening, shared food and worship. I live at a new Quaker community, where we're beginning to welcome Friends for short stays and retreats. Most people find me a bit odd – I'm vegan, don't drive or fly, and often wear shorts as I hardly heat my home and find most buildings too hot. For me the key sustainability challenge is changing the way we live and engaging the spirit of the age within and around us, with its focus on individual material consumption. Quakers have a particular contribution in our experience of finding unity in complex, difficult situations: listening, seeing God in the other, and thinking it possible that we might be mistaken.

In my work as a teacher, the most significant change I have experienced since becoming a Quaker has been the ability to be silent and to listen, I mean really listen; not just to what is being said but to the voice of that of God in them. It may seem strange and even spooky to think like that but it has helped me enormously in getting students to reveal more of themselves and to work more harmoniously with colleagues. Many of the international students I work with really appreciate and need the pastoral care I give. Sitting in silence in meeting for worship has brought out the reflective side in me and helped me become more attuned to the needs of others.

My working life was spent mainly on NHS finance, and it was easy to feel that the doctors, nurses, porters and cleaners on the front line were doing a more valuable job. But I came to realise what a huge difference it made to them if finance was handled well. So when, after retiring, I became a Quaker and was immediately recruited to be the meeting's treasurer, it felt good. The way we handle our money enables the meeting to flourish, and also facilitates great things, from Britain Yearly Meeting's work worldwide to some tiny charities run by our own members. Indeed, without a lot of backroom work there would be no meetings, no outreach, and for that matter no hospitals. Backroom work is important, and this has wider implications.

If I never want to resort to violence, then I have to work to eliminate the seeds of war from my life in every way possible. For example, if I buy clothes that are made in sweatshops then I am complicit in economic violence, so instead I buy my clothes from charity shops and mend them as much as possible. But I also have to try to eliminate the violence and injustice that is perpetrated by the state on my behalf. This has led me to write a guide on how to disrupt arms company recruitment on university campuses, to being arrested for blockading the entrance to a nuclear weapons base, to taking part in Camp for Climate Action to highlight the injustice and damage of climate change, to lawsuits, lobbying and legal observing to counter police repression, and to not a lot of free evenings and weekends! Quakerism for me is not about an hour on Sunday, it is about every moment of your life. It is not comfortable, easy and conformative; it is a radical challenge to our whole way of life and society around us.

There are groups with a Quaker connection that you can join as soon as you start attending a meeting and many others with charitable status that you can help either with money or as a volunteer. Here is a selection, more or less at random: Quaker Action on Alcohol and Drugs; Quaker Arts Network; Quaker Asylum and Refugee Network; Quaker Concern for Animals; Quaker Congo Partnership; Quaker Fellowship for Afterlife Studies; Nontheist Friends Network; Quaker Social Action; Quaker Truth and Integrity Group; Quaker Universalist Group; Quaker Voluntary Action. You will find a full list at https://www.quaker.org.uk/our-organisation/quaker-groups

Internationally, Quakers liaise with each other constantly, often under the auspices of the Friends World Committee for Consultation (www.fwccworld.org), sharing their knowledge and experience and frequently partnering with each other in peace building initiatives around the world. At the time of writing, British Quakers are active in Burundi, Rwanda, Kenya and Israel-Palestine. It is a constantly changing scene. For an update, visit the Quaker website (www.quaker.org.uk).

Quaker Council for European Affairs (www.qcea.org) has a permanent office at Quaker House in Brussels and works to express a Quaker vision in matters of peace, human rights and economic justice in a specifically European political context. Among many significant projects, it highlights problems which still remain in Europe with regard to the right to conscientious objection to military service, gathers data on the conditions of women in prison and works with members of the Council of Europe to promote economic justice, reconciliation and the right sharing of world resources. Its programme is large, impressive and constantly developing.

There are Quaker United Nations offices (www.quno.org) in New York and Geneva, where their representatives work for human rights, peace and disarmament, refugees, and global economic and climate justice. They have enjoyed a number of successful outcomes, one of the most impressive to me being on the question of the use of child soldiers in war – surely the most extreme example of officially approved violence towards children. Many agencies were involved in persuading the United Nations to make a declaration against it, but QUNO was one of the most active in initiating the process and drafting reports and briefing papers. Quakers are at their strongest when they work at a local level and move their experience forward for use in large projects; this was a classic example of it. In 2000, after years of complex negotiations, the UN General Assembly declared that 'states shall not recruit persons under the age of eighteen'.

Finally in this section, I can't resist quoting again from *Quaker faith and practice*. The writer is Pierre Ceresole, a Swiss Quaker who founded Service Civil International in the 1920s, an organisation dedicated to the rebuilding of poverty-stricken and war-torn villages worldwide:

> *You say: 'But with the best will in the world, I can't get to the point of believing in God.' Well then, if you want to believe in him, if you feel something great behind it all and not just words, well, work for God, and you will see not only that it comes to the same thing as believing in him, but something infinitely more alive, more real, more powerful which fills you and satisfies you more than anything you might vaguely imagine under the name of 'real and living faith' – a reality, a life and not words.*

Quakers and You

Quakers in the seventeenth century were condemned and imprisoned as heretics. Modern dictionaries define a heretic as a 'holder of unorthodox opinions', so I suppose Quakers would still have to plead guilty today: trying to find that of God in everyone is not an orthodox thing to do. Read to the end of the definition, though, and you arrive at the source of the word. It comes from the Greek *hairetikos*, meaning 'able to choose'.

Quakers can choose. They have never felt hidebound by tradition or dogma. Many of them are characterised by a startling open-mindedness. They exercise discipline in their lives, as they always have, but nothing is imposed on them. And yet I'm still not sure they necessarily feel they are always the ones doing the choosing. 'Attending to what love requires of you' can make unexpected demands. Being guided by the Spirit is not quite the same as thinking for yourself.

At the beginning of this book, I said that I wasn't trying to convert you. As we reach the end, it seems a good idea to repeat it. I'm not. What this book has aimed to do is explain a little of who Quakers are and leave the rest to you. They don't claim to have the answers. What they have are some very good questions. In fact, Quakers question everything. And it's your job now as a heretic, as someone with a choice, to question the Quakers and decide whether any of this works for you. It's your faith and your truth that matter. If, like me, you find the meeting for worship a fulfilling experience or if, like me, you find the quiet wisdom of particular Quakers to be a help in your life, you may want to stay a little. You will be made welcome.

Epilogue

You don't get converted into a Quaker; you gradually come to realise that you are one, usually because other Friends start treating you as one.

GERALD PRIESTLAND, 1978

In my first weeks of experiencing the subtle beauty of Quaker meetings, I wanted to be there as often as I could. It wasn't that I had to, or needed to, or even that I was determined to. Nor was it fanaticism. It was just that for the first time in my life I was able to express gratefulness. I kept going back, because Quakers allowed me a space in which I could thank God for my life.

They put no pressure on me to stay. I asked once or twice if they wanted me to pay anything or sign my name or show that I meant it, but they said no, they were happy to welcome me as long as I felt like coming. After about a year, an old hand fixed me with a friendly stare over his cup of tea. 'You do realise that if you turn up as often as this, someone's going to ask you to do a job,' he laughed. He was right: it happened three months later. Someone said, 'Would you serve on the Children and Young People's Committee?' I was doubtful, but I knew they must have considered it carefully, so I said yes. As it turned out, I enjoyed being part of that little knot of Quakers and accepting the tasks and learning about the decision making. I began to give what money I could to collections for the central work and the meeting house funds. Slowly it seemed that there was a place for me among these people.

It was three years or more before I considered joining the Religious Society of Friends. I thought, 'Well, why be a member? The worship is the same. There are no privileges or perks, no promotion. Quaker work is Quaker work and you can be an essential part of it whether you join or not. A lot of meetings don't let you be a clerk or a pastoral Friend or an elder, but those jobs take up time and I don't have much of that.' A month or two into my third year, I met a woman who had been going to meetings ten times longer than I had. 'I won't join,' she said, 'because I'm sure they'll ask me to take on something that's a burden or a bore.' I nodded agreement. Then, an hour or two later, I felt a pang of uncertainty. I thought, 'Aren't we both missing the point? It's just about being available, isn't it? And open? And knowing that these are people we want to be associated with? That we want to help?' Looking back, I think it was the moment that I was able to come out as a Quaker to other people. Perhaps I also needed to come out as one to myself.

There are some who believe that you can be a Quaker without joining. I don't entirely share their view, but I think I understand it. Part of the Quaker identity is an attitude, a passion: you can undoubtedly have those without putting your name on a list. And it isn't an exact condition, like the measles. There's no kissing of rings, no initiation ceremony, no moment at which you acquire sudden quakerliness. But in the same way that you can catch the measles, it's certainly possible to catch Quakerism. And some time in that third year, I got it. It bit deep. I began to understand that I could be a Quaker in my way and that if I tried to emulate someone else's brand of Quakerism, I wouldn't be a Quaker. I realised that I needed, just for myself, to be able to say in public that I had taken a decision to change. And I felt – and still feel – that, while it's possible to do that without joining, it helps to know that there are committed people prepared not only to be on a list, but to declare themselves so nourished by the Religious Society of Friends that they want to nourish it back.

I hesitated for weeks. It was a big step. I mentioned it to loved ones and quickly changed the subject. I don't think they understood why it was so hard to talk about. I don't think I did. But it felt like a life-changer. Then, one day, something happened as I finished a telephone call. I'd been talking to a member of my meeting, an easy conversation, just a simple bit of business. I put the phone down and, without a moment's thought, pulled a sheet of paper from the drawer. I scribbled a one-line letter to the Membership Clerk as if I had suddenly learned the art of automatic writing. 'Dear Sheila,' it said, 'I would like to apply for membership of the Religious Society of Friends.' Nothing else. I signed it, stamped it and sighed with relief. It wasn't my problem any more. The Quakers could sort it out now.

The ways in which they sorted it out I found to be gentle and beguiling. The procedure has been the same for many years, a mixture of the formal and informal, of the general and particular. When you express interest in becoming a member, Quakers initiate a process whereby they simply get to know you better. It is your Area Meeting that you will be joining, so your local pastoral Friends formulate a plan of action which is intended to help everyone – principally you, but also members of the Area Meeting, whom you may not know well – to be sure that you understand what membership involves. In theory there's an infinite number of ways of achieving the same result; in practice most meetings tend to use one method more regularly than the others.

There are three routes frequently suggested. The first is a Meeting for Clearness, in which you and a group of Quakers come together to talk about what joining might mean to you. Or your meeting might propose a period, not fixed and possibly lasting a few months, during which you meet regularly with a small group of Quakers, who get to know you and with whom you can speak freely about everything. And the third option, well-established now, is that they ask two Quakers (one of whom you know well, the other from a different meeting) to visit you, so that you have an opportunity to talk things over in detail.

It is a system that works. It is based on the Quaker principle of encountering one another in the Spirit. George Fox put it well: 'Friends, meet together and know one another in that which is eternal, which was before the world was.' The procedure, whichever form it takes, is one in which people seek to understand the things that make each other tick: the experiences that have significance for them and the journey that has made them who they are. I'll never forget the warmth and care that characterised my own process. I was visited by two Quakers, one of whom I knew, the other a complete stranger. From the beginning of our couple of hours together, I felt in safe hands. These people were my guides. The discussion we had was open, thoughtful and wide-ranging. And it quickly became clear that this was my time. I asked questions and explored the whole business of my Quakerism just as much as they did.

A fragment of the conversation will give you a sense of it. With a modicum of guilt, I told them I was having trouble with two of the Quaker testimonies. Peace and simplicity, I said, were areas in which I thought I was messing up, so perhaps they ought to know. For example, I wasn't at all sure what I thought about conscientious objection; and I was living a tangled life, entirely lacking in simplicity, that just didn't seem right to me. If it had been an exam I would have been taking a risk, but I knew by then that this wasn't an exam. And now, years later, I still feel the affection I felt then for the clarity of their response. They helped. They met my uncertainty with their own experiences of trying and sometimes failing to live out the testimonies. They talked with ease of the speed with which things can change when people open themselves up to a life led in the Spirit. We discussed how Quakers' lack of dogma allows them to grow; how, by contrast, the shame of not feeling up to the mark blights healthy lives. By the end of the meeting we knew each other better.

A few days later, I heard that the Area Meeting had considered my application and that I was a member of the Religious Society of Friends. I was a Quaker. I felt good about that. I also felt responsible. Something I had always known in theory now came forcefully into my head as a big, important practicality. We members of the Society are *it*. *It is us*. If it's true that we're all the clergy, then it's also true that we own the buildings, change the light bulbs, put up the posters, hold meetings for worship, paint the walls, lobby governments and do all the other work that Quakers have done for centuries. It is our Society of Friends. There are thousands of us, so we don't have to feel our responsibility as a weight, but we do need to feel it as a vital element of our religious lives. Running the Quakers in Britain has a pivotal role to play in the life of everyone who joins.

I've called this book *Being a Quaker*, because I've tried to cover all aspects of a multi-faceted word: it can mean different things to different people. If you want to go to Quaker events and enjoy the wealth of spiritual fulfilment on offer, think of this book as *Being Someone Who Loves Quaker Meetings*. If you want to be involved with the running of your local group but don't feel ready to commit yourself to membership, call it *Being a Valued Attender of Real Importance to Your Meeting*. Quakerism incorporates all that. *Being a Quaker* means friendship of a kind and quality that you may only rarely find elsewhere. It means a faith that expresses itself in what you do, not what you think. It means the freedom to speak for yourself. It means the security of knowing that others are with you in the Spirit, and the understanding that you have a silent space in which to listen for the still, small voice. *Being a Quaker* is attending to what love requires of you; knowing one another in that which is eternal; seeking to answer that of God in everyone.

Appendix 1

What Next?

Considering their reputation for silence, Quakers can be a vociferous bunch. They talk and write constantly. In this book I've only managed to explore the shallows of a deep religious faith. If you want to know more, you have a lot of choices.

A good place to start is the Britain Yearly Meeting website (www.quaker.org.uk). You can find your nearest Local Meeting there, read the whole of *Quaker faith and practice* online (https://qfp.quaker.org.uk), watch film clips, contribute to the online forum and become absorbed in a rich fund of material about Quaker life and work. All Area Meetings have a web presence, too, so a little research may yield detailed information about the meetings near you.

If it interests you to widen the scope a little, the same vast website contains a number of features and stories, including the reparations Quakers are making for the transatlantic slave trade and colonialism indulged in by Quakers during the eighteenth and nineteenth centuries (https://www.quaker.org.uk/resources/reparations), and the work Quakers currently do for peace and social change (https://www.quaker.org.uk/resources/newsletters/quaker-faith-in-action). And there's much more. I suggest you follow your nose.

While you're at the computer, a search of www.youtube.com could be useful – at the time of writing, you'll discover a series of short films in which British Quakers talk about their faith. Much new material will be added in the future. You may also want to try one of the many Quaker blogs. I'd love to recommend some favourites of mine, but my experience has been that they tend to come and go rapidly, so any reference I give is likely to be out of date before this book is published. I hope you'll go online and explore.

There's a free weekly online update of news, views, events and discussion called *Quake!,* which gives a good sense of modern Quakerism in action. To sign up, go to: https://www.quaker.org.uk/resources/newsletters/quake .

If you're ever in London, you might pay a visit to the Quaker Centre (quakercentre@quaker.org.uk: 173 Euston Road, NW1 2BJ, 020 7663 1030). As well as an excellent café, they have a lively bookshop and a worship space. If you can't make it in person, their outreach team is available to email at outreach@quaker.org.uk or phone at 020 7663 1017. Get in touch and they will be happy to send you a free pack of Quaker material for newcomers. If you're particularly interested in material for young people, do be sure to specify that in your request.

If you want to explore young people's resources yourself, you might want to spend a little time at https://www.quaker.org.uk/communities/children-and-young-people-2/i-work-with-children-and-young-people-in-a-quaker-setting/resources-children._From that page I warmly recommend *Quaker Meeting and Me* and *Let's Explore the Quaker Way*, two small booklets aimed at the under-sevens. And I must also mention a warm, thoughtful little book intended for the same age group, but with something to offer people of all ages: *Peaceful Inside* by John Lampen (Independents United Ltd, 2013).

Woodbrooke (www.woodbrooke.org,uk) is an international Quaker learning and research organisation offering online courses in a large variety of subjects of interest to Quakers and newcomers. Their 'Woodbrooke Where You Are' programme offers visits from their tutors to Quaker meeting houses, and they also organise residential courses and one-day events in a number of venues across Britain. Full details are on their website.

A huge number of books is published about Quakerism. Some are for newcomers. Many more are written by Quakers for Quakers, but you may still find those worth reading for the insights they provide into the openness and diversity of the Religious Society of Friends. Chief among them are *Advices and queries* (Appendix 2 of this book, but available free as a pocket-sized booklet at the Quaker Centre and many meeting houses) and *Quaker faith and practice* (London: The Yearly Meeting of the Religious Society of Friends in Britain [Quakers], 5th edition, 2013).

No two introductions to Quakerism are alike, so if you're interested, I suggest you read at least one other. My personal favourite is Jim Pym's *Listening to the Light* (London: Rider Books, 1999). It was written pre-internet so it's a little dated now, but its format, taking *Advices and queries* as its theme, is original and engaging. I have also a produced another introduction with a different slant, *What Do Quakers Believe?* (Winchester: Christian Alternative Books, 2019), and a third suggestion in this category, though it's less an introduction to Quakerism than a joyous honouring of it, is Ben Pink Dandelion's *Celebrating the Quaker Way* (London: Quaker Books, 2009).

If you go to https://thekindlers.org.uk/booklets you will find a long list of excellent small books for Quakers at all stages of their religious development. Two that I particularly recommend are *Quaker Worship: Reflections and Explorations* by

James McCarthy and *Through Us, Not From Us: Vocal Ministry and Quaker Worship* by Rex Ambler, Alec Davison, Janet Scott and Michael Wright. And there are many more.

The Quaker Quicks series of short books contains an extraordinarily diverse range of modern Quaker writing. They are published by Christian Alternative, an imprint of Collective Ink Books. I suggest you peruse their list which, at the time of writing, comprises twenty-six titles covering different aspects of Quakerism: https://www.collectiveinkbooks.com/christian-alternative-books/our-books/jhp-search-results/?txt=quaker+quicks

Quakers mount an annual lecture (the Swarthmore) which anyone can attend and for which there is always an accompanying book. Some of the greatest Quaker writing is to be found in the many Swarthmore Lectures of the past, so it would be invidious to give too much emphasis to any in particular, but I can't omit *Costing Not Less Than Everything: Sustainability and spirituality in challenging times* by Pam Lunn (London: Quaker Books, 2011) which I have already recommended in Part Two. And here are four more of my personal favourites to give you a flavour of their variety: *What Canst Thou Say?* by Janet Scott (London, Quaker Books, 2007); *Openings to the Infinite Ocean* by Tom Shakespeare (London: Quaker Books, 2020); *Ground and Spring* by Beth Allen (London: Quaker Books, 2007); and *The Amazing Fact of Quaker Worship* by George Gorman (London: Quaker Home Service, 1973; reprinted by Quaker Books, 2010).

The last of those is a thoughtful reflection on the inner life and power of Quaker meetings. It's friendly, well written and authoritative, if a little dated now. And there's another book on worship that deserves a special mention: John Punshon's *Encounter with Silence* (Richmond: Friends United Press,

2006), a deeply personal account of one man's spiritual search seen through the lens of his discovery of Quaker worship.

If you want to read about Quaker peacemaking, two more Swarthmore Lectures stand out: *Peace is a Process* by Sydney Bailey (London: Quaker Home Service, 1993) and *True Justice* by Adam Curle (1981; 2nd ed. London: Quaker Books, 2007). If you're interested in conscientious objection and the reasons for it, I've never read a more thought-provoking or impassioned challenge to the institution of war than Diana Francis' *Rethinking War and Peace* (London: Pluto Press, 2004).

History is well represented in Quaker publishing. A fine, compact account is John Punshon's *Portrait in Grey* (1984; 2nd ed. London: Quaker Books, 2006). Another good source is *The Quakers: A Very Short Introduction* by Ben Pink Dandelion (Oxford University Press, 2009), which gives a clear rundown of the essentials and provides a helpful overview of the different strands of world Quakerism. If you prefer a more academic approach, looking at Quakers in their theological and sociological context worldwide, then try the same author's *An Introduction to Quakerism* (Cambridge University Press, 2007) which has a similar agenda, while being fuller and more complete.

Readers who want to immerse themselves in Quaker literature of the past might start with the selections in *Quaker faith and practice* (see above): as well as some fine religious writing, they will discover a host of possibilities for further exploration. Those who want to engage with the thoughts of early Quakers could move on to two outstanding spiritual autobiographies. *The Journal of George Fox* and *The Journal of John Woolman* are both available as glossy paperbacks, but the easiest and cheapest way to purchase them, if you have the technology, is as e-books.

George Fox in particular, though, can be a challenging read and so Rex Ambler's *Truth of the Heart* (2001; London: 2nd ed. Quaker Books, 2007) comes as a godsend. He has chosen extracts from Fox's work and reordered them, so they speak the author's message more clearly to modern readers; he has also provided idiomatic 'translations' from the original seventeenth century English on each facing page. If you're interested in Fox's complex character, *George Fox & the Quakers* by Cecil Sharman (London: Quaker Books, 1991, reprinted 2008) is the perfect starting point.

You may also be interested in a guided anthology for newcomers that I have compiled, with selections ranging from 1652 to modern times, entitled *The Spirit of the Quakers* (New Haven, CT, and London: Yale University Press, 2010).

There is a weekly magazine, *The Friend* (www.thefriend.org), and a quarterly journal, *Friends Quarterly* (for subscriptions and other queries, contact subs@thefriend.org). There are also many other magazines published by special interest groups of British Quakers.

Finally, a word about the publishers of this volume: Discovering Quakers is a charitable organisation that exists to help people curious about Quakers to find out more. Their website publishes articles, blog posts, videos and podcasts, as well as advertising events organised by Quakers. Once a week they host an online session called Quaker Lives, when a Quaker talks about how being a Quaker has enriched their life, and there's an opportunity to ask questions and sample a short meeting for worship. If you want to try an in-person meeting, they will help you to get in touch with the nearest one to you. You may like to pay them a visit at www.discoveringquakers.org.uk.

Appendix 2

Advices and queries

1. Take heed, dear Friends, to the promptings of love and truth in your hearts. Trust them as the leadings of God whose Light shows us our darkness and brings us to new life.

2. Bring the whole of your life under the ordering of the spirit of Christ. Are you open to the healing power of God's love? Cherish that of God within you, so that this love may grow in you and guide you. Let your worship and your daily life enrich each other. Treasure your experience of God, however it comes to you. Remember that Christianity is not a notion but a way.

3. Do you try to set aside times of quiet for openness to the Holy Spirit? All of us need to find a way into silence which allows us to deepen our awareness of the divine and to find the inward source of our strength. Seek to know an inward stillness, even amid the activities of daily life. Do you encourage in yourself and in others a habit of dependence on God's guidance for each day? Hold yourself and others in the Light, knowing that all are cherished by God.

4. The Religious Society of Friends is rooted in Christianity and has always found inspiration in the life and teachings of Jesus. How do you interpret your faith in the light of this heritage? How does Jesus speak to you today? Are you following

Jesus' example of love in action? Are you learning from his life the reality and cost of obedience to God? How does his relationship with God challenge and inspire you?

5. Take time to learn about other people's experiences of the Light. Remember the importance of the Bible, the writings of Friends and all writings which reveal the ways of God. As you learn from others, can you in turn give freely from what you have gained? While respecting the experiences and opinions of others, do not be afraid to say what you have found and what you value. Appreciate that doubt and questioning can also lead to spiritual growth and to a greater awareness of the Light that is in us all.

6. Do you work gladly with other religious groups in the pursuit of common goals? While remaining faithful to Quaker insights, try to enter imaginatively into the life and witness of other communities of faith, creating together the bonds of friendship.

7. Be aware of the spirit of God at work in the ordinary activities and experience of your daily life. Spiritual learning continues throughout life, and often in unexpected ways. There is inspiration to be found all around us, in the natural world, in the sciences and arts, in our work and friendships, in our sorrows as well as in our joys. Are you open to new light, from whatever source it may come? Do you approach new ideas with discernment?

8. Worship is our response to an awareness of God. We can worship alone, but when we join with others in expectant waiting we may discover a deeper sense of God's presence. We seek a gathered stillness in our meetings for worship so that all may feel the power of God's love drawing us together and leading us.

9. In worship we enter with reverence into communion with God and respond to the promptings of the Holy Spirit. Come to meeting for worship with heart and mind prepared. Yield yourself and all your outward concerns to God's guidance so that you may find 'the evil weakening in you and the good raised up'.

10. Come regularly to meeting for worship even when you are angry, depressed, tired or spiritually cold. In the silence ask for and accept the prayerful support of others joined with you in worship. Try to find a spiritual wholeness which encompasses suffering as well as thankfulness and joy. Prayer, springing from a deep place in the heart, may bring healing and unity as nothing else can. Let meeting for worship nourish your whole life.

11. Be honest with yourself. What unpalatable truths might you be evading? When you recognise your shortcomings, do not let that discourage you. In worship together we can find the assurance of God's love and the strength to go on with renewed courage.

12. When you are preoccupied and distracted in meeting let wayward and disturbing thoughts give way quietly to your awareness of God's presence among us and in the world. Receive the vocal ministry of others in a tender and creative spirit. Reach for the meaning deep within it, recognising that even if it is not God's word for you, it may be so for others. Remember that we all share responsibility for the meeting for worship whether our ministry is in silence or through the spoken word.

13. Do not assume that vocal ministry is never to be your part. Faithfulness and sincerity in speaking, even very briefly, may open the way to fuller ministry from others. When prompted

to speak, wait patiently to know that the leading and the time are right, but do not let a sense of your own unworthiness hold you back. Pray that your ministry may arise from deep experience, and trust that words will be given to you. Try to speak audibly and distinctly, and with sensitivity to the needs of others. Beware of speaking predictably or too often, and of making additions towards the end of a meeting when it was well left before.

14. Are your meetings for church affairs held in a spirit of worship and in dependence on the guidance of God? Remember that we do not seek a majority decision nor even consensus. As we wait patiently for divine guidance our experience is that the right way will open and we shall be led into unity.

15. Do you take part as often as you can in meetings for church affairs? Are you familiar enough with our church government to contribute to its disciplined processes? Do you consider difficult questions with an informed mind as well as a generous and loving spirit? Are you prepared to let your insights and personal wishes take their place alongside those of others or be set aside as the meeting seeks the right way forward? If you cannot attend, uphold the meeting prayerfully.

16. Do you welcome the diversity of culture, language and expressions of faith in our yearly meeting and in the world community of Friends? Seek to increase your understanding and to gain from this rich heritage and wide range of spiritual insights. Uphold your own and other yearly meetings in your prayers.

17. Do you respect that of God in everyone though it may be expressed in unfamiliar ways or be difficult to discern? Each of us has a particular experience of God and each must find the way to be true to it. When words are strange or disturbing

to you, try to sense where they come from and what has nourished the lives of others. Listen patiently and seek the truth which other people's opinions may contain for you. Avoid hurtful criticism and provocative language. Do not allow the strength of your convictions to betray you into making statements or allegations that are unfair or untrue. Think it possible that you may be mistaken.

18. How can we make the meeting a community in which each person is accepted and nurtured, and strangers are welcome? Seek to know one another in the things which are eternal, bear the burden of each other's failings and pray for one another. As we enter with tender sympathy into the joys and sorrows of each other's lives, ready to give help and to receive it, our meeting can be a channel for God's love and forgiveness.

19. Rejoice in the presence of children and young people in your meeting and recognise the gifts they bring. Remember that the meeting as a whole shares a responsibility for every child in its care. Seek for them as for yourself a full development of God's gifts and the abundant life Jesus tells us can be ours. How do you share your deepest beliefs with them, while leaving them free to develop as the spirit of God may lead them? Do you invite them to share their insights with you? Are you ready both to learn from them and to accept your responsibilities towards them?

20. Do you give sufficient time to sharing with others in the meeting, both newcomers and long-time members, your understanding of worship, of service, and of commitment to the Society's witness? Do you give a right proportion of your money to support Quaker work?

21. Do you cherish your friendships, so that they grow in

depth and understanding and mutual respect? In close relationships we may risk pain as well as finding joy. When experiencing great happiness or great hurt we may be more open to the working of the Spirit.

22. Respect the wide diversity among us in our lives and relationships. Refrain from making prejudiced judgments about the life journeys of others. Do you foster the spirit of mutual understanding and forgiveness which our discipleship asks of us? Remember that each one of us is unique, precious, a child of God.

23. Marriage has always been regarded by Friends as a religious commitment rather than a merely civil contract. Both partners should offer with God's help an intention to cherish one another for life. Remember that happiness depends on an understanding and steadfast love on both sides. In times of difficulty remind yourself of the value of prayer, of perseverance and of a sense of humour.

24. Children and young people need love and stability. Are we doing all we can to uphold and sustain parents and others who carry the responsibility for providing this care?

25. A long-term relationship brings tensions as well as fulfilment. If your relationship with your partner is under strain, seek help in understanding the other's point of view and in exploring your own feelings, which may be powerful and destructive. Consider the wishes and feelings of any children involved, and remember their enduring need for love and security. Seek God's guidance. If you undergo the distress of separation or divorce, try to maintain some compassionate communication so that arrangements can be made with the minimum of bitterness.

26. Do you recognise the needs and gifts of each member of your family and household, not forgetting your own? Try to make your home a place of loving friendship and enjoyment, where all who live or visit may find the peace and refreshment of God's presence.

27. Live adventurously. When choices arise, do you take the way that offers the fullest opportunity for the use of your gifts in the service of God and the community? Let your life speak. When decisions have to be made, are you ready to join with others in seeking clearness, asking for God's guidance and offering counsel to one another?

28. Every stage of our lives offers fresh opportunities. Responding to divine guidance, try to discern the right time to undertake or relinquish responsibilities without undue pride or guilt. Attend to what love requires of you, which may not be great busyness.

29. Approach old age with courage and hope. As far as possible, make arrangements for your care in good time, so that an undue burden does not fall on others. Although old age may bring increasing disability and loneliness, it can also bring serenity, detachment and wisdom. Pray that in your final years you may be enabled to find new ways of receiving and reflecting God's love.

30. Are you able to contemplate your death and the death of those closest to you? Accepting the fact of death, we are freed to live more fully. In bereavement, give yourself time to grieve. When others mourn, let your love embrace them.

31. We are called to live 'in the virtue of that life and power that takes away the occasion of all wars'. Do you faithfully maintain our testimony that war and the preparation for war

are inconsistent with the spirit of Christ? Search out whatever in your own way of life may contain the seeds of war. Stand firm in our testimony, even when others commit or prepare to commit acts of violence, yet always remember that they too are children of God.

32. Bring into God's light those emotions, attitudes and prejudices in yourself which lie at the root of destructive conflict, acknowledging your need for forgiveness and grace. In what ways are you involved in the work of reconciliation between individuals, groups and nations?

33. Are you alert to practices here and throughout the world which discriminate against people on the basis of who or what they are or because of their beliefs? Bear witness to the humanity of all people, including those who break society's conventions or its laws. Try to discern new growing points in social and economic life. Seek to understand the causes of injustice, social unrest and fear. Are you working to bring about a just and compassionate society which allows everyone to develop their capacities and fosters the desire to serve?

34. Remember your responsibilities as a citizen for the conduct of local, national, and international affairs. Do not shrink from the time and effort your involvement may demand.

35. Respect the laws of the state but let your first loyalty be to God's purposes. If you feel impelled by strong conviction to break the law, search your conscience deeply. Ask your meeting for the prayerful support which will give you strength as a right way becomes clear.

36. Do you uphold those who are acting under concern, even if their way is not yours? Can you lay aside your own wishes

and prejudices while seeking with others to find God's will for them?

37. Are you honest and truthful in all you say and do? Do you maintain strict integrity in business transactions and in your dealings with individuals and organisations? Do you use money and information entrusted to you with discretion and responsibility? Taking oaths implies a double standard of truth; in choosing to affirm instead, be aware of the claim to integrity that you are making.

38. If pressure is brought upon you to lower your standard of integrity, are you prepared to resist it? Our responsibilities to God and our neighbour may involve us in taking unpopular stands. Do not let the desire to be sociable, or the fear of seeming peculiar, determine your decisions.

39. Consider which of the ways to happiness offered by society are truly fulfilling and which are potentially corrupting and destructive. Be discriminating when choosing means of entertainment and information. Resist the desire to acquire possessions or income through unethical investment, speculation or games of chance.

40. In view of the harm done by the use of alcohol, tobacco and other habit-forming drugs, consider whether you should limit your use of them or refrain from using them altogether. Remember that any use of alcohol or drugs may impair judgment and put both the user and others in danger.

41. Try to live simply. A simple lifestyle freely chosen is a source of strength. Do not be persuaded into buying what you do not need or cannot afford. Do you keep yourself informed about the effects your style of living is having on the global economy and environment?

42. We do not own the world, and its riches are not ours to dispose of at will. Show a loving consideration for all creatures, and seek to maintain the beauty and variety of the world. Work to ensure that our increasing power over nature is used responsibly, with reverence for life. Rejoice in the splendour of God's continuing creation.

More books about Quakers by Geoffrey Durham

What Do Quakers Believe?

Publisher: Christian Alternative
ISBN: 978-1-78535-893-7

"So what do you believe?" It's the question Quakers are always asked first and the one they find hardest to answer, because theirs is a religion of doing, not thinking. They base their lives on equality and truth; they work for peace, justice and reconciliation; they live adventurously. And underpinning their unique way of life is a spiritual practice they have sometimes been wary of talking about. But they hold many beliefs in common – and there has never been a Quaker publication that sets them out as clearly as Geoffrey Durham does here. He answers the question in the title straightforwardly and without jargon. In the process he introduces a unique religious group whose impact and influence in the world is far greater than their numbers suggest.

> *'The clearest introduction to Quakers I have read. Beautifully and clearly written, this book brings Quakerism to life in a very accessible way.'*
>
> Nick Baines, Bishop of Leeds,
> writer and broadcaster

The Spirit of the Quakers

Publisher: Yale University Press
ISBN: 978-0-300-16736-8

In *The Spirit of the Quakers* Geoffrey Durham introduces Quakerism through the words of the Quakers themselves. This book is a guided anthology, featuring quotations from writings that cover 350 years, from the beginnings of the movement to the present day. Peacemaking, simplicity, truth, and equality are major spiritual themes, but there are also beautifully written pieces describing Quakers' wide diversity of belief, their collective values, their insistence on taking action for social change and their understanding that we can all answer 'that of God in everyone'. Start at the beginning and read through to the end and you will understand the essentials of the faith through the words of some of the most eloquent Quaker writers of all time.

'I can't recommend this book clearly enough. It is captivating.'

TERRY WAITE CBE, WRITER AND BROADCASTER